CHARLIE ONE

Seán Hartnett was born in Cork in 1975 and is married with two step-children. He joined the British Army in 1998 and served for almost seven years before moving first to South Africa, then Australia and finally returning to Ireland just as the Celtic Tiger was collapsing. He has worked as a security consultant for major companies and on government projects worldwide. He has also worked in the area of commercial espionage and counter espionage. He is a fanatical rugby fan and is a sucker for a slice of good Tiramisu.

CHARLIE ONE

THE TRUE STORY OF AN IRISHMAN IN THE BRITISH ARMY AND HIS ROLE IN COVERT COUNTER-TERRORISM OPERATIONS IN NORTHERN IRELAND

SEÁN HARTNETT

MERRION
PRESS

Published in 2016 by
Merrion Press
10 George's Street
Newbridge
Co. Kildare
Ireland
www.merrionpress.ie

© 2016 Seán Hartnett

British Library Cataloguing in Publication Data
An entry can be found on request

ISBN 978-1-78537-085-4 (Paperback)
ISBN 978-1-78537-086-1 (Kindle)

Library of Congress Cataloging in Publication Data
An entry can be found on request

Design by Sin É Design
Typeset in Minion 12/14 pt
Front cover by www.phoenix-graphicdesign.com
Cover images © Pacemaker Press International (paramilitary) and
© Andrey Popov | Dreamstime.com (CCTV bank)
Printed and bound in Great Britain by TJ International Ltd.

For the brave men and women of JCU-NI,
especially for North Det and Cameras Section.
Ní Bheidh ár Leithéidí Arís Ann.

Go out into the highways
and along the hedges
and compel them to come in
so that my house may be filled.

JCU-NI motto (Luke 14:23)

CONTENTS

NOTE TO THE READER

For security reasons many of the names and locations in this book have been changed. Identifying some of those involved on both sides may put their lives at risk. Those who are mentioned have already made it into the public domain with regard to the events featured in this book and further prior involvement with the Troubles in Northern Ireland.

The naming convention of the JCU-NI personnel used in this book is unique to JCU-NI. It was used for both security purposes and for ease of remembering people's names and functions at the Det. The convention was simple, your first name followed by the Det's slang term for your job description i.e. Seán Tech (Royal Signals technician), Colin Opso (operations officer), Brian Ops (operator) or Mandy Spook (intelligence officer). It was part of a unique language spoken at the Det and became second nature to me during my time there.

MAP OF NORTHERN IRELAND

0 10 20 30 40 50
Scale   Kilometres

Innishowen

Lough Foyle

Ballycastle

Coleraine

Ballymoney

Limavady

Shackleton Barracks, Ballykelly - North Det

Sheriff's Mountain

Letterkenny

Derry/ Londonderry

Dungiven

ANTRIM

DONEGAL

LONDONDERRY

Ballymena

Larne

Strabane

Francis Hughes Arrest Site

Maghera

Newtownstewart

RAF Aldergrove South Det, 7 SCT, SAS Interceptor Unit

Moscow Camp

Bangor

Cookstown

Lough Neagh

Belfast

Palace Bks. Holywood East Det

Omagh

TYRONE

Andersonstown

Coalisland

Lisburn

Dungannon

Belleek

Ballygawley

Loughgall SAS Ambush site

Lurgan

Craigavon

Thiepval Barracks JCU-NI HQ

Lower Lough Erne

Portadown

Enniskillen

Abercorn Barracks Ballykinler

FERMANAGH

Lough Erne

Armagh

DOWN

Monaghan

ARMAGH

Newtownbutler

Newry

MONAGHAN

CAVAN

Carrick-on-Shannon

Cavan

Dundalk

LOUTH

Drogheda

Navan

Mullingar

Athlone

Dublin

MAP OF DERRY CITY

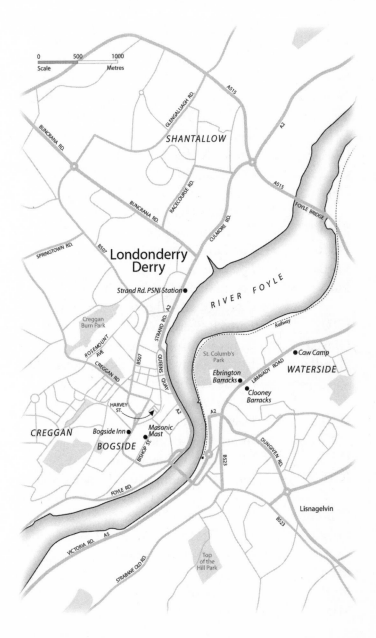

GLOSSARY OF TERMS

AOR	Area of Responsibility
ASU	Active Service Unit
Bleep	Slang term for a Royal Signals radio operator at a JCU-NI Det
Box	MI5
Brownie	Slang term for a photographer attached at a JCU-NI Det
CIRA	Continuity IRA
CMOE	Covert Methods of Entry
CO	Commanding Officer
Det	Slang term for a JCU-NI outpost, short for 'Detachment'
ELINT	Electronic Intelligence
FLIR	Forward Looking Infra-Red
FMB	Forward Mounting Base
FoS	Foreman of Signals – Warrant Officer in charge of all technicians at a unit
FRU	Force Research Unit
GPMG	General Purpose Machine Gun
Handler	British Army Intelligence Officer who handles informers within paramilitary organisations
HMG	Heavy Machine Gun
IED	Improvised Explosive Device
IVCP	Illegal paramilitary checkpoint
JCU-NI	Joint Communications Unit-Northern Ireland
JTF-HQ	Joint Task Force-Headquarters
LEWT	Light Electronic Warfare Troop
LVF	Loyalist Volunteer Force
MLA	Member of Legislative Assembly
MOD	Ministry of Defence
MRF	Military Reaction Force

NCO	Non-Commissioned Officer
NLJD	Non-Linear Junction detector
OC	Officer Commanding
OOB	Out of Bounds
PIRA	Provisional Irish Republican Army
Pronto	Slang term for a Royal Signals NCO in charge of all radio communications at a JCU-NI Det
PSNI	Police Service of Northern Ireland
RCG	Regional Co-ordination Group
ROE	Rules of Engagement
RPG	Rocket-propelled grenade
RSM	Regimental Sergeant Major
RUC	Royal Ulster Constabulary
RUF	Revolutionary United Front
SAS	Special Air Service
SBS	Special Boat Service
SCT	Special Communications Troop
Shakey	Slang term for an SBS Trooper serving at JCU-NI
SLA	Sierra Leone Army
Spanner	Slang term for a Royal Electrical Mechanical Engineer (mechanic) at a JCU-NI Det
Spook	Slang term for an Intelligence Corps officer at a JCU-NI Det
Squadron OC	Officer Commanding Squadron
Sugar	Slang term for an SAS Trooper serving at JCU-NI
TCG	Tasking and Co-ordination Group
TSCM	Technical Surveillance Counter-Measures
UDA	Ulster Defence Association
UDR	Ulster Defence Regiment

PROLOGUE

HOW THE HELL DID I END UP HERE?

It was approaching 2100 hours on Sunday, 17 February 2002, and darkness had settled in completely over Northern Ireland. Three Tyrone men – Donald Mullan from Dungannon, and Seán Dillon and Kevin Murphy, both from Coalisland – moved blindly through a field in Coalisland, carrying what we suspected was an RPG 22 rocket launcher complete with warhead, something they were later acquitted of in court. A fourth – Brendan O'Connor from Pomeroy – sat in a grey Peugeot car in a nearby car park. They had target designations of 'Charlie One' through to 'Charlie Four' and were suspected members of an East Tyrone Real IRA active service unit.

Though they didn't know it at the time, they were not alone that night and had not been for quite some time. JCU-NI operators, combined with SAS (Special Air Service) and SBS (Special Boat Service) troopers, had had the four men and the location under intense surveillance for over a week before this. And the darkness made no difference to them now: they had night-vision capabilities as part of their kits. So too did the two video-surveillance cameras positioned in the surrounding ditches, beaming images forty miles away to the operations room in Shackleton Barracks, Ballykelly, where the operations officer sat in front of his bank of monitors, ready to give the order.

As for me, I was four miles from the action, watching it all on my own personal 'feed' from the surveillance cameras and closely monitoring the radio network for signs of trouble. I was a nervous wreck and wondering to myself how the hell I had ended up in this situation, me, an innocent fella from Cork caught between sympathising with the nationalist community in the North and helping the British army outsmart its enemy.

1 UP THE 'RA

The Sinn Féin office in Cork city at that time was located on Barrack Street, just across from a pub called Nancy Spain's, which was a favourite drinking haunt for us UCC students. In spite of my naivety, I wasn't daft enough to just walk in there and ask to join the IRA. I actually did a bit of digging first and got the name and phone number of a local Sinn Féin figure whom I was told would be able to help. We arranged to meet on a Sunday morning in April 1995.

I got up that morning having spent the whole night going over in my head what I was about to do. I had never been in trouble with the law, hadn't even had so much as a bad report home from school, and yet here I was with a half-baked plan to join one of the most notorious terrorist organisations in the world.

The closer the time came to leave for the meeting, the more insane the idea seemed.

*

There weren't many clues in my past that I would end up where I did.

I was born in 1975 in a small village in Co. Cork, into a family of six girls and three boys, a good Irish Catholic family. In the old days, as the youngest son, I might have been sent off to join the priesthood.

Back in November 1968, my parents had returned to Cork from London, where they had met and married two years previously. They were both from families whose roots were firmly in Cork and it was practically inevitable that they would end up there themselves. My oldest brother was the only one of us to be born outside Ireland, the rest of us were Cork-born and bred.

My father got a job in the booming textile industry that had sprung up all over the county, and seemed set for life. Unfortunately, though, it didn't last, and in 1981 he was made redundant. That was the last proper job I remember him having: he spent the rest of his days on the dole, occasionally picking up some work on the fishing boats, either with his brother or another crew, but it was never steady work. In these circumstances, like so many other men of that era, he took to drinking, and the responsibility of providing for the family fell to my mother. She worked a variety of cooking, cleaning and secretarial jobs over the next thirty years, and it was all down to her that we got by and that my siblings and I all managed to get decent educations.

Growing up in the 1970s and 80s in Ireland was tough; money was tight and with so many mouths to feed my mother often struggled to make ends meet. As it continued, my father's drinking sapped the family finances – a fact that never seemed to bother him much, and we were often left hungry. Each of my older brothers and sisters had a part-time job from an early age and their wages were used to supplement my mother's meagre income. My turn came too; I took my first job at twelve years old, working two hours a day after school and a half-day on Saturdays in a fish co-op, where my two older brothers had also worked. It was tough going but I loved it; the craic was always good and my wages of £20 a week, stuffed into a brown envelope, I handed over to my mother with pride. Many of the families on our small housing estate, one of the many built as part of the government social housing initiative, were in the same boat, so we didn't stand out. We had the advantage of having great neighbours, with everyone pitching in to help each other out; and forty years on, they remain just the same.

My home life, however, was not so happy or supportive; my father was argumentative with drink on him. He was the classic street angel, house devil, and as a result many of my early years were spent outdoors with others of my age, escaping his influence. This was before the days of Xbox and PlayStation, and we made your own fun out in the fields and woodlands that surrounded the village. On free days, we would head off at first light, only returning for meals and sometimes not even then. I loved the outdoors and in fact was just as happy out wandering about on my own as I was surrounded by friends. There may have been a soldiering seed planted in those days; but of course a seed needs more than planting.

Things came to a head with my father one night when he came home with drink on him. I was sixteen years old, and as usual he was being an ass, picking fights with anyone who would take the bait. That night it was I who bit, and out of a sense of frustration and perhaps a desire to stand up for those who couldn't defend themselves as well, I landed a punch square on his jaw, sending him to the floor. I had been a karate student with the local club since I was eleven, training two or three times a week, and I knew how to throw a punch. It would be the first of many fights between us over the next few years, with family members often having to intervene to keep us apart. Looking back, I think it might have been an urge to right things, to intervene to try to sort things out once and for all. Most of all, though, I think I just hated bullies. It's been almost twenty-five years since that night, and I have never spoken a word (other than in anger) to my father since. My parents separated some years later, and while the rest of the family have stayed in close contact with him, my antipathy towards him remains.

Like every other boy in our village, I was educated by the Christian Brothers both in primary and secondary school. I was a bright student and so managed to avoid the wrath of some of the sterner brothers. I loved studying history, in particular Irish history: the accounts of Michael Collins, Éamon de Valera and the Easter Rising sparked my imagination, and from there I became a prolific reader of Irish history. By that time, of course, the Troubles in Northern Ireland were at their worst, with Provisional IRA bombing campaigns spreading to the UK and Loyalist murder squads operating across the North. I became fascinated by it, and had a sense of watching history unfold before my eyes on the TV screen and in the newspapers every day.

I sat my Leaving Certificate in 1993 and got enough points to study science at UCC. In truth, I had little interest in the subject, but I jumped at the chance to get away from home, which at that point had become unbearable. I would have taken any option open to me. My first year at university went well, I enjoyed the freedom that came with living away from home for the first time and made good friends. I passed my first year exams without any problems but by the second year I was spending more time at history lectures with my friend Norah than at my own science ones. It was one day during a laboratory session towards the end of that year that I looked around and just knew that it was no longer for me. The thought of spending the rest of my life cooped up in a lab was too much to take. Breaking the news to my family was, I thought at the time, one of the hardest things I would ever have to do. But actually, there were even harder things ahead.

Looking back at the uncertainty I created in my life at that stage, I realise now how lucky I was to have got to where I am today. It could have been very, very different if I'd gone through with my first plan.

The origins of that plan probably go back to 8 May 1987, when British Special Forces killed eight PIRA (Provisional Irish Republican Army) volunteers at Loughgall, Co. Armagh. One of those killed on the day was Seamus Donnelly, aged just nineteen. He was a neighbour and first cousin of my uncle's wife, who was from a staunchly Republican area and a staunchly Republican family. My family therefore felt close to what had happened. I could feel the anger in the room as we watched the news reports, and it created a hatred in me from an early age for 'the Brits'. Needless to say, we only saw how these men had been butchered under an SAS shoot-to-kill policy, not how their plan to murder RUC officers had been sabotaged.

This wasn't my family's only link to Northern Ireland, either. Another uncle had married into a Republican family from Carrickmacross, and an aunt had married a man from Castleblaney in Co. Monaghan, near the border. Like most Irish families we were very close to our uncles, aunts and cousins, and through those connections with the North we grew up hearing many stories of British army raids on homes and of the oppression of the Catholic population in Northern Ireland.

My first plan, stemming from all this, was to join the IRA and the fight to get the British out of the North and reunite the country. I knew that was the idea, but I hadn't actually put much thought into it. It was more that I found myself swept along by romantic notions of being a freedom fighter, fighting for justice against an evil oppressor, and this was the nearest such opportunity to home. The reality of actually blowing people up and taking someone's life, and living with the consequences, hadn't registered fully in my young mind.

Fortunately, on the day I was due to start the process of joining up, I bottled and didn't go to the meeting. Luckily, too, I hadn't told a soul what I had been planning, so I didn't have any explaining to do.

CHARLIE ONE

Where did that leave me? I had left university and was working in a factory. Although the money was good and I had moved into a house with some friends, I wasn't happy. The thoughts of settling down in a small town and spending the rest of my days in a mundane job began to frighten me. I longed for travel, adventure and a greater sense of purpose.

I decided to join the army.

2 THE QUEEN'S SHILLING

Word was out now that I was leaving home and moving to the UK. I had told everyone I had a job with British Telecom and most people took that at face value. The night before I was to take the train, there was a bit of a party in the local pub with family and friends. It was not the American wake of old, but it did involve lots of drink and generally trying to avoid sadness of all kinds.

I never liked goodbyes, myself, so the next morning I got up and left earlier than planned, slipping away quietly to start my new life.

*

Unfortunately, upon further investigation I realised that in the Irish army I would probably end up doing cash escorts, border duty or UN peacekeeping, and that was enough to put me off the idea.

Meanwhile, however, during the space of two weeks in February 1996 the IRA planted bombs at Canary Wharf, Charing Cross and Aldwych in London, killing three people, including one of their own members, and injuring countless others. Three of my sisters were now living in London, as well as many friends and relatives, and the bombing proved to be a major reality check for me. Worried for my sisters' safety and finally realising the terrifying nature of all terrorism, the romantic idea I had of the Republican movement disintegrated.

My thoughts turned to doing something about it: to

joining the British army and fighting against terrorism, the very terrorism that only a year earlier I was considering contributing to. Travel would be assured, I reasoned; adventure would be likely; and perhaps even the chance to do something good might come my way.

But how could I possibly do so, given my family background? Paradoxically, I realised that my father had actually served in the RAF for a number of years himself, and my mother had worked as a secretary for the British Ministry of Defence (MOD) before they moved back to Ireland. My grandfather, too, I'd heard, had served with the British army during World War II. Slightly ironic, I realised, but no one ever seemed to have had a problem with it, so why should they have a problem with me doing the same now?

Nonetheless, I didn't tell anyone of my plans at first, and spent a good few months just thinking it through. Then in April of 1997 I wrote a letter to the British army careers office based in Belfast, enquiring how I should go about joining up. A month later, I received a reply. It turned out that joining up as a citizen of the Republic was going to be a slower process than I'd expected, but I sent off the application form and waited.

And waited. And waited.

About six months later, in October 1997, I got a letter instructing me to attend my first interview the following month at St Lucia Barracks in Omagh. The instructions were very precise: I was to get the bus from Dublin to Omagh, make my way to the Silverbirch Hotel, and check in under the name given to me in the letter. It all seemed a bit over the top to me, but I went along with it willingly.

The journey from Cork to Dublin and then on to Omagh was uneventful, but I did find myself suddenly more interested in the British army towers and patrols I saw as I crossed the border. I had never seen so many armed police and soldiers; the IRA must have been more active than I thought, I reasoned.

Somewhat self-consciously, I checked into the Silverbirch Hotel that evening. I was to be at the main door the following morning at 0900 hours to be picked up and taken to the interview. I was hungry, though, so I popped down to the hotel bar to grab a bite to eat. I ordered a steak and a pint of Guinness, careful not engage in conversation with anyone as I felt I should stay inconspicuous. How foolish I felt then when I was settling the bill and the barman asked me straight out: 'Ready for your interview tomorrow?' I was like a deer caught in headlights and he laughed: 'It's okay, son, they all stay here before they go over.' I went back upstairs to my room, double-locking and chaining the door, convinced that the IRA could well be coming for me.

The following morning, outside the door of the hotel, a car pulled up beside me and a guy with a Northern accent yelled out the window: 'Hartnett?'

Jesus, I thought, was this guy trying to get me killed? I was still a little skittish from the previous night's episode and stood there in shock for a few seconds until he eventually shouted again, 'Get into the fucking car, will ya, or we'll be late!'

I jumped into the passenger seat and, much to my surprise and amusement, I barely had the seatbelt on when we drove up to the entrance of the camp. It was right across the road from the hotel.

In the waiting room there were about ten other candidates, and I stuck out like a sore thumb; not because of my background, though, but because – brought up by my mammy – I had gone to the trouble of dressing in a suit and tie. Everyone else was in jeans or a tracksuit. How was I ever going to fit in? I wondered.

At least I didn't have to sit there for too long. Since I had the furthest to travel home, I was first in.

The interviewing officer was a captain in the Argyle and Southern Highlanders and a jovial enough guy.

'So why the British army?' was his first question. Upfront and personal, I think he was going for!

I replied with the reasons I had prepared: family connections to the British Armed Forces, my wish to travel, etc. He seemed happy enough. Then threw me a curveball.

'How do you think you'll manage as a Catholic in a Protestant army?'

I turned it back on him without batting an eyelid.

'I didn't realise the British army was a Protestant force. I thought it was non-denominational.' He smiled at me.

'Good answer! You'll hear from us in due course with a date for your second interview and fitness test. In the meantime, keep training and stay out of trouble!'

It wasn't until the following January that I got another letter to attend the same barracks in Omagh for my fitness test, aptitude tests and final interview in February. It was time to tell the family. Even though I worried and fretted about it, their reaction couldn't have been better: they were only concerned for my safety, especially with what was happening in the North.

'You won't be posted to the North, though, will you?' my mother asked.

'Of course not,' I assured her. How was I to know!

We agreed it was best to keep it to ourselves for the time being.

The fitness test involved a 1.5-mile run, two minutes of sit-ups and two minutes of press-ups. I had been training for months beforehand and was well able for it. I did the run in less than ten minutes, and managed a hundred press-ups and a hundred sit-ups. I didn't have any problems either with the aptitude test or the final interview, and in fact I did so well they were suddenly offering me the choice of any military trade I wanted. With some help from the recruitment staff, I decided to train as a radio technician with the Royal Corps of Signals, which would give me a decent trade when I eventually left the army.

And that was it. I was to become a member of the British Armed Forces.

Six weeks later I got news of my starting date for training. I was to register on the first of September at Palace Barracks in Holywood, Co. Down.

My family was very worried now; just two weeks previously, the Real IRA had killed twenty-nine people and injured more than 200 with a bomb in Omagh. It was the single biggest loss of life in the Troubles. Whatever about my family worrying, I was more determined than ever now to sign on the dotted line.

I arrived at the train station in Belfast and a driver was there with my name on a card. He drove me to Palace Barracks. I was expecting some sort of ceremony as I took the Oath of Allegiance to the queen, but there was no such thing. I was taken into a room with an army officer and given a piece of paper to read from. Where were the bands and the parading soldiers? There was just a picture of the queen hanging on the wall and that was it. I read the words aloud as instructed. They sounded hollow to me and even though they were only words, something didn't feel right about it. My heritage, my Republican upbringing and my years of observing the Troubles from that perspective were objecting to what I was doing. But it was too late.

I was driven to Belfast City Airport and put on a flight to start my basic training and take the Queen's Shilling.

3 SWIFT AND SURE

It was a Friday afternoon when I arrived home and, after the initial family time, I took the short walk to the local pub in search of my first pint in four months. There was the usual collection of locals propping up the bar. I made my way to the back of the lounge and stood alone waiting to be served. I spotted the owner, Maureen, as she moved up the bar towards me. I had known her all my life and she never seemed to age a day in that whole time.

'Guinness, Seán?' she asked.

'When you're ready, please, Maureen.' As she pulled the pint she looked me square in the eye and asked: 'So how is the British army treating you?' She smiled while my jaw dropped. 'There are no secrets in this place, Seán, you should know that. You needn't worry, though, no one here will have anything to say about it and if they do they'll have me to answer to.' Over the years I had seen this woman face down drunken men twice her size with no more than a stare and would rather face down a soldier than Maureen any day.

I realised, however, that I'd need to be on my own guard despite Maureen's assurances.

*

Army Training Regiment, Bassingbourne, was where my life in the army began, with four months of phase-one, basic military training.

If I thought there was a lack of ceremony at Palace Barracks, then my arrival at Bassingbourne was positively anticlimactic. Picked up by a military driver at the train station in Royston, I was deposited at my troop accommodation block without so much as a glance from the hundreds of other troops scurrying around the vast camp. My section corporal took me into a room and promptly searched the two bags I had brought with me. I was allowed to keep one set of civilian clothing, sportswear, socks and underwear. The rest I was assured I wouldn't be needing for the next four months. I was marched (though that's probably too technical a word for it) into the troop office where I was introduced to my troop sergeant, Sergeant Carter. Carter was the stereotypical British army sergeant, a huge barrel-chested man, with a moustache, and a pace stick permanently tucked under his arm. I instantly liked the guy. He was to the point and tolerated no bullshit.

'Right, Hartnett, I see you're from the Republic. Nobody here gives a shit. Any problems with the other recruits: officially, I want to hear about it. Unofficially,` sort it out yourself!'

I was then led down the corridor to my section room. As we entered, one of my fellow recruits called the room to attention. I was impressed. The room consisted of ten bed spaces. Each had a single bed complete with army-issue blankets and sheets, a fitted wardrobe, chest of drawers and a footlocker. The beds faced one another in an otherwise open room. Only one space was empty, and this, I realised, would be my home for the next four months.

'Right, Paddy, get your kit unpacked and be quick about it. Everyone outside in three ranks in two minutes!' the section corporal roared as he left the room. No one had time to introduce themselves to me, such was the panic to get outside. Panic would be a regular state for us all during our first few weeks, as we struggled to get used to the relentless pace of army life. And Paddy would be my nickname for my first eighteen months of army life. It's just how it was: if you were Irish you were Paddy, if you were Welsh you were Taff, and if you were Scottish you were Jock. There were many other nicknames used depending on where you came from or what you looked like, but no offence was ever intended or taken. Everyone accepted it as the army way.

First stop for every new recruit is the regimental barber. As we filed into the less than stylish room that served as the barber's salon, Sergeant Carter cheerfully informed us, 'You can have any haircut you like, as long as it's a number one all over.' Once everyone had the identical haircut, we headed to the squadron quartermaster. There we were kitted out with uniforms, boots, bergens and webbing, everything we would need for life as a soldier. After those preparations, the routine began.

Our days were defined by 0500 starts, with physical training of one sort or another at least three times a day interspersed with room and kit inspections, drill parades and, most important of all, weapons training and tactics. We never walked anywhere, it was always on the double and always carrying weight. I loved the physical aspect of soldiering, whether it was on a booted run, loaded down with a Bergen full of sand, or multiple trips over the assault course in full combat gear. I had thought myself fit when I had signed up, but I wasn't actually 'military fit'. I soon was, though.

It wasn't just fitness, either. By the end of my basic training I could strip, clean and reassemble an SA80 assault rifle or general-purpose machine gun (GPMG) blindfolded. This wasn't some pointless exercise that the training staff made us do for shits and giggles, but rather an essential part of being able to operate effectively as a soldier at night. We were taught that darkness was often a soldier's best friend, so we had to be able to operate in it.

The map-reading and the survival skills that we learned meant that we could operate independently for extended periods of time. We learned how to manoeuvre in a firefight, carry out snap ambushes and section attacks. We learned how to give short and sharp orders using voice projection and hand signals, a vital skill amidst the noise and confusion of battle.

Over that sixteen-week period I went from a somewhat scrawny figure to a much leaner, stronger and more resourceful creature I barely recognised. Irrespective of what trade we planned to pursue, we were soldiers first and foremost, and the military training staff certainly did their job well of breaking down the civilian in us and building us back up as soldiers.

The four months of basic training flew by, with only a single weekend off in that whole time. Unlike the other recruits, I couldn't return home that weekend as the security vetting procedure to travel to the Republic wouldn't allow it for such a short time. Instead, I headed for London where some of my siblings were living.

Spending twenty-four hours a day together with the other recruits meant we became very close friends, and I remain in contact with many of them to this day. But you can't be friends with everyone, and I was on course for a showdown of some sort from the start with one particular recruit. He was a Scottish lad from Glasgow, a die-hard Rangers supporter, and he took an instant dislike to me. Over that first couple of weeks, he goaded and baited me with calls of 'Fenian bastard', 'Filthy Taig' and suchlike. I bit my tongue at first, but eventually enough was enough. I knew I could never beat him in a fair fight as he was twice my size. Just as well I didn't fight fair! I stood ironing my kit one evening and he started at me, this time shoving me from behind as the insults came. I swung full force with the red-hot iron and caught him square on the chest, knocking him to the floor. The iron had come out of the socket, and I stood there with it over him, ready to deliver another blow. 'You're fuckin' crazy! You could have scarred me!' he screamed. I must have had a look of madness in my eyes as I whispered, 'Next time, I'll bury it in your face and you'll never be able to forget me.' The funny thing is, from that day on we became firm friends for the rest of our army careers. That's just the way soldiers dealt with things.

The day of the passing-out parade arrived and spirits were high amongst the whole troop. There were three awards up for grabs: best shot, best physical training and best recruit. I was given best physical training, and with the other winners presented myself in front of the Commanding Officer (CO) on the parade square to accept the award. Many of my family travelled from Ireland and London to see the ceremony, and as we marched out on to the square in full ceremonial dress, accompanied by the pipes and drums of the band, I must admit I felt ten feet tall.

My basic training complete, I had two weeks' Christmas leave. It would be my first time in the Republic as a British soldier, and for the army that wasn't a trifling matter. For two weeks prior, I had been allowed to grow my hair, and soon looked like a civilian again. But that wasn't enough. I was summoned to a briefing by the security intelligence officer the day before my leave was due to start. The briefing was long, tedious and more than a little patronising. I was assured the threat to me while at home in Cork was quite real, and got a lot of advice how to prepare for it: 'Do not pack your clothes in a military hold-all for your trip home. Do not take anything military home with you. Do not tell anyone you are in the British army or discuss with anyone any details of your service.' Best of all was: 'Do not associate with any Republican or paramilitary organisations while home on leave.' It was as if they took me for a complete idiot, yet this briefing would be given to me time and again throughout my military career.

Once that was over, I left ATR Bassingbourne never to

return. I made my way to Heathrow Airport for the flight home. One of the great things about serving in the British army was the free travel warrants you got when going on leave, four per year. Both my train journey to Heathrow and my flight to Cork were paid for in full by the British army.

As it was Christmas, I bumped into many old friends over that two-week period and it was during those encounters that I discovered just how much I had changed. Many people had commented on the change in my physical appearance, but it was the change in me as a person that I now noticed. I was no longer interested in village life, local politics, who was seeing who, and the usual local scandals. It wasn't that I felt above it, just different. I had an itch that needed to be scratched. I was so anxious to get going that two days before my leave was due to end I took an early flight back to Heathrow and on to the next stage of my British army career at the Royal School of Signals in Blandford, Dorset.

The telecommunications course I had chosen was one of the best trades in the Royal Signals, reflected in the fact that at the end of the course you were promoted to lance corporal and the highest pay grade in the army. It was thus, not surprisingly, also one of the longest training programmes.

I spent just over a year at Blandford learning my trade. In the beginning, the course was just like any other college electronics course. We studied applied maths, physics, electronic principles, analogue and digital circuits and transmission systems. It was when we moved on to the practical phase of the course that things got more interesting. We would be met every morning at the entrance to the secure wing of one of the dozens of training buildings on the vast camp. Once signed in, we would be escorted at all times until we were signed out again in the evening. It was in those secure wings that we learned how to test and repair every radio and communications system in the

British army, everything from Manpack radios to tank-borne systems. We also learned to deal with the most precious of all systems, cryptography. Technicians had a unique insight into this vital component of British army communications because not only did we need to be able to use it but also to repair it.

As you'd expect in the army, we had the odd parade, but in general we were there to learn the trade. We worked Monday to Friday but had most weekends off. I took up boxing and cross-country running to make the most of my spare time. I stayed fit and firmly focused on my career throughout. Our moto, after all, was *Certa Cito*, Swift and Sure.

At the end of the training, the issue of which army unit I would join had to be decided. I submitted a list of my top three choices with no guarantee I would get any of them. Most of my mates went for postings like Cyprus, Germany and London, where they could enjoy extra money and a great social life and little chance of seeing action. That approach wasn't for me. I wanted a unit I could travel with and see the world, even if it was some hellhole. I reasoned that there were two things the army never went anywhere without, no matter how big or small the contingent: satellite communications (21st Signal Regiment) and an electronic warfare unit (14th Signal Regiment), so I put both on my list. I got 14th Signal Regiment, which wasn't that surprising considering no one else wanted it.

Located at Brawdy army base in south-west Wales, 14th Signal Regiment wasn't known for being a glamour posting. The isolated location of the base and the harsh Welsh weather made it uninviting, but it proved a great posting for me. First, we only worked a four-day week, which enabled me to pursue one of favourite hobbies: hillwalking. With the Brecon Beacons less than an hour's drive away, I spent most weekends there with a few mates, crisscrossing the peaks, and following it up with a few well-earned pints. I kept up boxing, and I was able to take an advanced course in jamming technology (used to disable enemy communications) so as to improve my chances of being deployed: jammers are often deployed in support of other units.

All in all, I wasn't complaining about Brawdy, but by mid-2000 I was getting a little bored with the predictable life of the base. I wanted some adventure. The opportunity came sooner than I'd expected.

4 SIERRA LEONE

While all the fighting was going on, back at our operations room we listened in to the very controlled and professional communications of the assault force, and what a contrast that was to what we heard from the rebel ranks. As they tried desperately to defend themselves and communicate what was going on across their network, our jammers did their thing and rendered the attempts at communication useless. This generated further panic and helped significantly in the success of the mission.

*

In May 2000, 226 Squadron's Light Electronic Warfare Troop (LEWT) was readying for a deployment to Sierra Leone, which was in the grips of a vicious ten-year civil war. Despite having vast mineral wealth, the country remained one of the poorest on the planet thanks to decades of war and corruption. The Sierra Leone Army (SLA) and government was led by President Kabbah. The anti-government rebels, the Revolutionary United Front (RUF), led by 'Brigadier' Foday Sankoh, were marching on the capital, Freetown. Trying to keep the two sides apart was the UN peacekeeping force, UNAMSIL, but it was far too under-resourced to be able to hold back the rebels. Tony Blair decided to dispatch a rescue force to extract British and other foreign nationals to safety. The mission, codenamed Operation Palliser, involved 800 men from the Parachute Regiment, led by the force commander brigadier,

David Richards, and was meant to last between seven and ten days. Fifteen years later, there are still British troops in Sierra Leone.

The LEWT was a small troop, composed of about a dozen men from my regiment, 14th Signals, and they were mainly deployed with British Special Forces to provide communications, direction-finding, interception and jamming capabilities. Everyone in the LEWT was airborne-trained, and on this mission they would be deploying with the Parachute Regiment. As the rest of our regiment watched in envy, the LEWT guys moved about Brawdy camp in their stripped-down Landrovers fitted with 50mm heavy machine guns (HMG) and 7.76mm GPMGs. Kitted out in tropical warfare uniforms and jungle boots, they looked the part, and we envied them.

LEWT lacked only one thing: a communications and electronic warfare technician. However, before I could even throw my hat in for selection to join the mission, my mate Susan was chosen to deploy with them. I was gutted, of course, but quickly put it to the back of my mind and got on with my normal duties.

A few weeks after LEWT's initial deployment, our sergeant major appeared at the door of the tech workshop.

'We've received a further warning order for Sierra Leone,' he said, addressing Jock the tech sergeant. I was in like a shot, cocky as hell, immediately listing off the reasons why I should be part of the next deployment. He stood there, expressionless, until I finally stopped talking.

'Save your breath Paddy,' he said, 'you've already been picked. Get your ass down to the medical centre and sort out your jabs.' A warning order didn't necessarily mean that I would be going anywhere, just that we had to be ready to go at a moment's notice. No one knew for sure where the mission was headed at that point, and I knew it could well be over before I got a chance to deploy. Selfishly, I was probably one of the few people hoping that the British army presence in Sierra Leone would continue.

Over the next few weeks I watched anxiously and enthusiastically as Brigadier Richards stretched his initial rules of engagement (ROE) to push the RUF back into the jungle. On 26 May, 600 men from 42nd Commando took over from the Parachute Regiment, and on 15 June Operation Palliser officially came to an end, succeeded by Operation Basilica which aimed to train and support the SLA in defeating the rebel forces. I was overjoyed at the news as it would mean a long-term commitment to Sierra Leone. I was now certain of being deployed.

Within a few days I had begun training for my first overseas deployment to a combat zone as a British soldier. This involved everything from advanced weapon training and mine clearance to jungle warfare. We were given the general background to the conflict in Sierra Leone: how Sankoh's war effort was funded by the smuggling of unregulated diamonds, known as blood diamonds, across the border to neighbouring Liberia. Liberia was under the control of President Charles Taylor, who took the diamonds in exchange for drugs and weapons, which in turn fuelled the war.

There would be six of us from the regiment deploying as part of Operation Basilica, replacing the troops that went out initially. The day before we departed, we got our final briefing from one of the LEWT staff sergeants who had just returned from Sierra Leone. He didn't have anything good to say:

> 'First off, Sierra Leone is a shithole and I mean that in the worst possible way. There is no infrastructure to speak of. Mains electricity, clean water and sewerage systems are almost non-existent. However, on a good day you can, oddly enough, get great mobile phone coverage!

Like in many parts of Africa, child soldiers are part of the conflict. Be under no illusions: a round fired by a child will kill you just the same as a round fired by an adult. Don't hesitate, because they won't. Drink and drugs make the rebels utterly unpredictable, so never let your guard down ... One final thing: Freetown's largest-growing industries since the arrival of the UN forces are drugs and prostitution. They are known locally as 'night-fighters'. HIV, AIDS and every other STI you can think of are at epidemic levels in Sierra Leone, so don't even think about it.'

The following day we would collect our personal weapons from the armoury and board the flight for Lungi Airfield, Sierra Leone.

Due to the threat of ground fire as we approached Lungi, the pilot of RAF *Galaxy* made a very rapid descent and hit the pothole-marked runway with an awful thud. There was no doubt about it, we were now in a combat zone – fortified British army positions, checkpoints, and British and UN helicopters dotted all over the airfield. Nonetheless, the main thing I noticed as we alighted from the aircraft was the humidity. My light jungle warfare uniform was wet through within minutes.

We travelled the thirty miles to Freetown in a convoy protected by six weapons-mounted Landrovers manned by members of the Royal Irish Regiment. Sad-looking villages and an unending number of dilapidated roadside shacks lined the route, but it was the sight of the impoverished children chasing the convoy, hoping that food would be thrown by the soldiers, that hit me hardest. Reading about poverty and seeing it are two very different experiences.

As we approached the ferry point at Tagrin, I looked in

horror at what we were about to board. The lopsided rust bucket sitting with its ramp lowered on the quayside looked barely able to float itself never mind carry a full load of military vehicles and personnel across the mouth of the Sierre Leone River. After a tense and agonisingly slow voyage, we rolled off the ferry in the Kissy district of Freetown.

I was about to take a deep breath of relief when I got the stench from the open sewers and untreated sewage flowing freely in the streets. This was a city in free fall. Already bursting at the seams before the war, it was now entirely overrun with a population desperate for any sort of refuge from the rebel forces. They lived in makeshift houses, made of everything from plastic, timber and – for the lucky ones – corrugated steel. The buildings that had once been properly constructed from concrete were now scarred with shell and bullet marks and in otherwise terrible condition.

As our convoy arrived at the HQ of the SLA, where the British army Joint Task Force Headquarters (JTF-HQ) was also based, our vehicle peeled away and continued along another road until we arrived at the gates of Spur Lodge. This had once been a luxurious villa owned by some wealthy Freetown family. In more recent times it had been the HQ of the South African mercenary group, Executive Out-comes. (Talk about a euphemism!) Now it provided accommodation for the personnel from 14th Signal Regiment. The compound was surrounded by high walls and, thanks to Executive Outcomes, the building itself had bulletproof windows capable of stopping a 50mm round, and reinforced doors. Less comfortably, though, the place was covered in signs of bullet and shell strikes; it had obviously been under attack at some point in the not-too-distant past.

We settled in nonetheless. Our operations room was located in the nearby SLA HQ building, a very nondescript room. Its main feature was the reinforced steel door with viewing hatch. Two SLA armed guards were permanently stationed at the door. Inside we scoured the airwaves in search of RUF transmissions, did our best to pinpoint their locations, and where necessary render their communications useless with jammers. My job was to keep all the equipment running with the limited tools and spares I had at my disposal. My partner in crime was a signaller known as Mule, and between us we managed to keep things ticking along nicely.

Everything was routine enough for a while. Then, on 25 August a patrol of twelve Royal Irish Ranger soldiers, led by Major Alan Marshall, ran into trouble. They were carrying out a routine inspection in the Occra Hills, when despite the concerns of the SLA liaison officer, Lieutenant Musa Bangura, Marshall ordered the patrol off the main route into an area known to be controlled by a group of rebels referred to as the West Side Boys. (Marshall believed that the West Side Boys might now be willing to disarm and become part of the peace accord.) The group of about 300 rebels was mainly composed of renegade soldiers from the failed coup of 1997 and they were notoriously unpredictable. Deep in their territory, the patrol was stopped by a truck, mounted with an anti-aircraft gun and quickly surrounded by a group of the West Side Boys. After several demands from the rebels to drop weapons, Marshall, against standing orders, ordered his men to do so. Of course, they were immediately overwhelmed and taken hostage.

They were brought to Gberi Bana where the West Side Boys, led by 'Brigadier' Foday Kallay, were based. Kallay realised immediately that he had a very valuable commodity, but worse still he recognised his old comrade from the SLA, Lieutenant Musa Bangura. Over the next two weeks, while all the hostages were subjected to beatings and repeated mock executions, Kallay saved his worst for Musa Bangura.

During face-to-face negotiations with the West Side Boys, the signals officer, Captain Flaherty, managed to pass on a map of the compound, including the location of where the hostages were being held, to our negotiating team. This was our first breakthrough. Then, a few days later, Kallay released five of the hostages in return for a satellite phone: a serious error on his part. While the satellite phone allowed Kallay to communicate with both the British military and the BBC about his demands for political recognition and an amnesty for the West Side Boys, it also allowed us to pinpoint his exact location.

As the safety of the hostages was made increasingly uncertain by the erratic behaviour of Kallay and his drug-fuelled troops (including demands of free passage to the UK and university places!), a decision was made in JTF-HQ in Freetown to carry out a rescue mission, codenamed Operation Barras, and Mule and I were ordered to gather as much intelligence as possible on the West Side Boys' movements to help in the planning. When the Special Forces contingent from the SAS, SBS and the Parachute Regiment arrived, our little group took on an even more significant role in assisting them. With only six of us from the regiment deployed, it meant all hands to the pump.

SAS and SBS observation teams were in place for several days prior to the main attack and managed to pinpoint all enemy positions and the location of the hostages. The West Side Boys' main camp had approximately 150 men, with a further 100 located on the other side of the river, Rokel Creek. The two locations were to be attacked simultan-eously, with the SAS and SBS hitting Gberi Bana, where the hostages were held, and the Paras attacking Magbeni, the rebels' other village on the opposite side of the creek, to prevent the rebels there from supporting Gberi Bana.

On the morning of 10 September at 0630, the rescue team, led by D Squadron of the SAS and supported by members of the SBS and 140 men from the Parachute Regiment, left their base at Hastings, thirty miles south of Freetown. The assault helicopters headed towards Rokel Creek, while the SAS/SBS observation teams opened fire on the base. The supporting attack helicopters laid down covering fire on both villages, while the SAS/SBS troops fast-roped from the Chinooks.

As is usually the case, this assault didn't go entirely smoothly. The first setback occurred when the Paras dropped from the Chinook helicopters and found themselves chest-high in swamp that intelligence had failed to spot. As he hit the ground, SAS Trooper Bradley Tinnion was hit and, despite being medevac'ed to RFA Sir Percival, as we later discovered, died from his wounds. The second was that the rebels, spurred on by drink, drugs and the belief in voodoo magic, put up a much fiercer fight than anyone had expected.

For the rescue mission itself, which lasted less than thirty minutes, the official death toll for the rebels was twenty-eight killed and eighteen captured, including the leader, Foday Kallay. The assault force lost one man and had eleven others injured. However, the actual fighting continued long after the hostages had been freed, and according to the Paras and Special Forces we met after the attack, it was closer to 200 rebel forces killed and 150 captured. Clearly a message was being sent to other rebel groups that this was the British army in the field, not some rabble afraid to come after them. The message got through alright and it wasn't long after Operation Barras that the RUF signed up to a peace accord.

On my return from Sierra Leone, and now a corporal, I had, thankfully, to wait only a few months before I was deployed again, this time to Oman on Operation Saif Sareea II, the largest deployment of British forces since the Falklands War. The entire regiment was there, with only a skeleton staff being left behind at Brawdy. I went as part of the jammer force and looked forward to another adventure in a place that was totally new to me.

We weren't long in Oman when the attack on the Twin Towers in New York changed the security picture of the entire world. While it didn't alter the training exercise that we were part of, it did put the wheels in motion for units of our regiment to deploy to Afghanistan. I wanted to be part of that and knew the LEWT was gearing up to be on the first assault. I headed to the tent that acted as 14th Signal's HQ in the southern desert in Oman. I had only just entered when my squadron OC (Officer Commanding) spotted me.

'Forget it, Hartnett, you're not going. You're needed here to look after the jammer vehicles. End of story.'

That was that. I would spend the next three months in Oman thinking mostly about my next posting and where I might go.

5 NORN IRON

We turned a corner and were suddenly met by an IRA checkpoint: four armed and masked men manning a makeshift barricade. Everything we had been taught said that I should reverse at speed while my passenger laid down covering fire.

I was having none of that. Instead, I approached the roadblock very confidently and lowered my window.

'How a' you?' I enquired in my strongest Cork accent.

'Where the fuck are you going?' came the reply.

'Just heading for Derry. Working on the Limavady by-pass,' I replied very casually. The poor fella had no idea how to react and simply looked over at the instructor for directions. The instructor made his way to the checkpoint.

'What are you playing at, Seán?' he yelled, 'that's not how we practised it. You'd be dead by now.' My reply was calm and measured.

'I don't think so. I have the right accent and a plausible story; much better than trying to reverse out of here or get involved in a firefight. I can talk the talk about anything they can bring up and get away with it.' He stared at me for a couple of seconds, growled 'Your funeral', and walked off.

*

I was due a new posting that November and on my return from Oman I decided I'd like to go to Northern Ireland. It wasn't that I'd had enough of overseas deployments and wanted to go home for good. Far from it. But I had just bought my first home in Norfolk and the extra money and additional leave would be welcome for the next few years. I also felt it was time to play my part in the situation 'at home'.

Two of my fellow techs had already been posted to a unit called JCU-NI. Although at that point I hadn't heard of JCU-NI, I was familiar with names like FRU (Force Research Unit), 14 Intelligence Company and even The Det, from the many books I had read about collusion, death squads and covert operations in Northern Ireland. These somewhat shadowy bodies even made the headlines from time to time in the Irish media, mixed with the stories of British army units butchering IRA active service units and vice versa that we all heard from relatives up North. JCU-NI sounded interesting, and at least there would be a few friendly faces there to show me the ropes. The only thing I had heard from my mates that were already there was that it involved no uniform or rank to speak of, and there was additional pay, which all sounded good to me.

I approached the foreman of signals (FoS) about the plan.

'Are you joking, Hartnett? With your background? Whatever about one of the other Northern Ireland units, you haven't a chance in hell of being posted to JCU-NI, so put the idea out of your head!' The reaction and answer pissed me off. I was never one to be told I couldn't do something, so I decided to go over his head to the squadron OC, a major from Northern Ireland who I had served with in Sierra Leone. I chose the high-stakes approach and gave him an ultimatum: JCU-NI or I leave.

He nearly let me leave, I sensed, but at the time the army was in desperate need of experienced technicians, so after some heated discussion, he caved. 'All right, JCU-NI it is. They are going to have fucking kittens when you rock up, Hartnett.'

There was still no guarantee that I would get JCU-NI. That would be down to some clerk at manning and records in Glasgow. But sure enough, they came up trumps, and I was off.

I landed in Belfast City Airport on 16 November 2001, a fully trained, experienced and decorated British soldier since the last time I was there. I was headed for Thiepval Barracks, the HQ of JCU-NI in Lisburn, Co. Antrim. There I would hook up with two other Royal Signals technicians for initial training

I was met by Dave, my old mate from 14th Signal Regiment. He was leaning against his car and had a big cheesy grin on his face. I struggled a little to open the car door because of the weight of it and threw Dave a questioning glance. He didn't seem to notice. As we drove off, he took a pistol from his waistband and placed it in the pocket of the driver's door, as if for easier access.

'So, what's the story with this place, Dave? No one is telling me anything, other than it's a great posting.'

He laughed: 'You'll find out soon enough, mate.' The only thing I got from him was that once initial training was completed, we were each to be sent to a different section – Cameras, Radios or something called 'North Det'. The decision on where we would end up was yet to be made, or so we were told.

As we made our way from the airport to the barracks, he pointed out various sites where JCU-NI had 'assets' located; places like New Lodge, the Divis Flats, the Royal Victoria Hospital, Castlereagh police station, and Dunmurry. I actually had no idea what 'assets' he was talking about but nodded away just the same. We arrived at Thiepval where he drove me round to a series of Portakabins located at the far side of the base, well away from all the other accommodation blocks. Finally, he pointed to one in particular: 'This one's yours, mate. But don't get too comfortable. You might not be staying long!'

After I got cleaned up, we took a walk over to the tech

workshops, located in a secure compound surrounded by razor-topped fences and high gates. The reinforced door had an electronic keypad and was monitored, like the rest of the compound, by CCTV cameras. Once inside, Dave showed me into an office where he introduced me to Bob, the FoS, and Andy from workshops. Bob FoS was first to speak: 'Seán, good to meet you.' I instantly recognised his particular Belfast accent and my first thought was, oh fuck, this could be a problem! However, despite Bob's staunch Loyalist upbringing, he wasn't the bigot in the room. Andy Workshops was all smiles and full of good-humoured banter, but there was something I didn't trust about him and I soon learned that he had more faces than Big Ben.

It was a Friday afternoon and there was a leaving party up in the JCU-NI HQ building, so everyone headed there. It seemed like a good start to me. The nondescript, two-storey building that served as JCU-NI HQ had more to it than met the eye. The building, despite already being within a high-security British army base, was also discreetly guarded by heavily armed civilian officers. No vehicles were allowed to park anywhere near it. The windows were coated with an anti-surveillance film and were blast-proof. On entering the building through a normal-looking door, you were met with an inner steel door that was remotely opened by the duty signals operator once your identity had been confirmed and cleared. Non-JCU-NI personnel were never allowed inside the building under any circumstances.

Everyone who was armed unloaded their pistols and handed them in to the armoury before we made our way to the bar, which was already filling up. I was impressed with how lavish it was in comparison to other rooms. Beer in hand, I mingled a bit, bumping into a few mates I knew from other units who were now posted to JCU-NI. Before long, Andy Workshops grabbed me.

'Time for you to meet the boss! The CO [Commanding

Officer] and the RSM [regimental sergeant major] are the only ones you call "sir" here, by the way. With everyone else it's first names only. Never ask for anyone's surname.'

We made our way through the crowd until I was in front of someone clearly of a quite high rank, the tweed jacket and tie a dead giveaway.

'Sir, let me introduce Seán Hartnett, just arrived from 14th Signal Regiment today.' Andy was grinning and my instincts told me this wasn't a good thing.

'Pleased to meet you, sir. I'm looking forward to working here,' I said as I stuck out my hand to shake the hand the CO was already offering in greeting. His hand recoiled before I could get a hold of it.

'You must be fucking kidding me,' he blurted out on hearing my thick Southern accent. I later learned that the CO was a deeply religious man and rarely swore. Clearly his surprise was so great on this occasion that a swear got out. He regained his composure and apologised.

'Excuse me, Seán. I'm … I'm … I'm sure you've been properly vetted for this and are more than capable. I'm … well, just a little surprised to have a Southerner in this unit.'

'No problem, sir,' I replied in typical Irish fashion, 'I'm just as surprised every time I see a British soldier in Northern Ireland.' Both the CO and RSM laughed. Andy didn't see the funny side.

The bitter truth of the matter, though, was that I should never have been posted to JCU-NI. Yes, I fitted the technical requirements, but not the security profile, not for a black ops unit anyhow. (A black ops unit doesn't exist on paper and requires the highest level of security vetting.) Some clerk in the manning and records section in Glasgow must have simply seen the need for a radio technician at a unit called JCU-NI, and then seen my request to join the unit, and put the two together, oblivious to JCU-NI's true purpose and my possible ulterior motives for wanting to join it. It was a serious flaw in the system, reflecting one of the problems of conducting 'black operations' through a dummy unit: how can you integrate it with the 'normal' operations of the army?

I spent the next hour or so chatting with the CO. He was genuinely interested in why I had joined up and in my background (though I left out the bits that might have made things more awkward for me). Over the years that followed, I actually built up a great relationship with the man, and on a number of occasions he asked if I'd be interested in taking the operator's course. My answer was always the same: I knew my limits and was perfectly content being a technician.

Later that night Bob FoS sidled up to me.

'Look at us, an Ulster Prod and Free State Fenian working together. Who would have thought?' he laughed. 'I know what you're thinking, Seán, but I'm not the one to worry about. That fucker Andy Workshops thinks you shouldn't be here and he'll do what he can to get you out, so keep your nose clean!' Irrespective of the copious amount of alcohol we had both consumed, I believed him. Great, I thought, day one and I already had to watch my back!

The rest of that weekend was spent socialising with the other JCU-NI members at Thiepval, in particular the technicians from Cameras and Radios. One thing that became obvious was that none of the JCU-NI technicians fancied the idea of a 'North Det posting'. Every time it was mentioned, they'd laugh, pitying whichever of us three new boys ended up there.

The following Monday morning our training began, and my fellow technicians and I drew our weapons from the armoury, SIG sauer 9mm pistols and HK53 assault rifles, weapons normally reserved for British Special Forces units. I was starting to wonder why Royal Signals technicians were going to need such firepower. We headed to RAF

Aldergrove, a stone's throw from Belfast International Airport, where we were among about a dozen other JCU-NI new arrivals under the tutelage of three special-duty veterans. We spent the morning on the firing ranges, learning handling drills and how to zero the scopes of our new weapons. We then drove the forty miles to the base at Ballykinler in Co. Down. JCU-NI had a special area reserved at one end of the camp where they had a complete replica of a typical small Irish town.

First off, they gave us a demonstration of the devastating effects of an improvised explosive device (IED). About 500m from the reinforced observation bunker where we stood was a car with approximately four pounds of Semtex explosives attached to the underside. Before the bomb disposal officer pushed the switch to detonate the device, he informed us, 'This is one of the IRA's favourite booby-trap devices, used to kill police and prison officers, soldiers and Loyalist paramilitaries. Here's why you always check your vehicle for an IED.' No sooner had the words left his mouth than the car erupted in a ball of flames and was lifted from the ground like it was a toy. As it crashed back down to earth, all the chatter and jokes ceased and the grim realisation of what we risked hit us.

Over the next three days we ran through various scenarios we might find ourselves in while moving around Northern Ireland: paramilitary roadblocks, car hijackings, armed robberies, paramilitary punishment beatings, ambushes and suchlike. We also learned how to manoeuvre our modified vehicles, with their Kevlar armour plates fitted to the doors and seats, which made them a lot trickier to handle. (I suddenly understood the weight of the door on the car that Dave had collected me in.)

While my approach to some of the scenarios we trained for, including using my thickest Cork accent, perplexed the training staff, it was how I planned to deal with things here on my own turf, so to speak, so I wasn't for changing or apologising. I planned to use my Irish background to my advantage whenever possible. This strategy also came in handy for one of my operations officers.

6 HOWES AND WOOD

The only overt thing about our overt cameras was the fact that you could see them if you looked. Their true nature was actually extremely covert, highly classified, and one of JCU-NI's best-kept secrets.

These cameras could read a vehicle number plate clearly from 1.8km away. They could pan, tilt and zoom in any direction in a matter of milliseconds. Each had a number of pre-programmed positions, and a simple push of a number on the keyboard controller would send the camera to that position in an instant. Using state-of-the-art low-light technology, they could even 'see' in the dark. There was nowhere to hide.

Connecting the cameras was a vast network of encrypted fibre-optic cables spread throughout Northern Ireland for the exclusive use of British Intelligence. The encryption ensured that even if the feed from a surveillance camera was intercepted, it would be indecipherable. This allowed real-time control of feeds from all the JCU-NI's surveillance cameras.

Thanks to the distance between the camera locations and our 'targets', the paramilitaries didn't associate the cameras with surveillance. Over time, they ignored the overt cameras altogether. This was a huge mistake on their part since those distant lenses gave us constant 'eyes' on their stomping grounds, like the Creggan, Shantallow, Strabane, the Waterside and the Bogside.

Sitting in front of a vast wall of TV monitors in the operations room, fed by signals from this powerful network, *the operations officer(Opso) could track a vehicle or individual in real time from any point in the city to any other point, or manoeuvre his operators like chess pieces around the city, and indeed all the way down to the so-called 'bandit country' of South Armagh and Tyrone. As they dropped out on one camera they would be picked up by another, or by an operator; all the while oblivious to the level of surveillance they were under.*

*

There were three more modules to go in our technical training at JCU-NI, followed by an exam, before a decision would be made as to who would go where.

First was a riggers course at RAF Digby in Lincolnshire. To work as a technician at JCU-NI you had to have a head for heights. Rigging army cameras or radio antennas to public masts or buildings anywhere was challenging, what with hazardous weather conditions and awkward climbs. But in Northern Ireland there was the added difficulty of having to do all the rigging at night for security and tactical reasons. Even under cover of darkness, though, the chance of being hit by a firework or petrol bomb (some might even say by a gunshot, though that would be going too far in my experience) made working at JCU-NI even less appealing. If you failed your riggers course, you were out. Heights were never a problem for me and so I passed without difficulty. So too did the other two technicians.

The Cougar radio network was used by all British army units in Northern Ireland, including JCU-NI. There were, however, significant differences in what was available to JCU-NI through the network and what a normal unit had. Whereas normal units would experience dead spots where no radio communications were available, this wasn't the case for JCU-NI. They had a series of signal boosters, known as 'high powers', placed strategically in military bases and police stations to enhance their network and prevent dead spots in communications. They were completely unknown to other units. There was also the fact that all JCU-NI communications equipment was covert in both appearance and function.

Finally, there was the Cameras section, covering JCU-NI's vast network of overt CCTV cameras. Of course, JCU-NI weren't the only ones using CCTV cameras in Northern Ireland. Everyone from commercial companies protecting their premises, local council authorities trying to stamp out antisocial behaviour, private individuals, and the RUC created an ever-increasing number of CCTV cameras. This posed a problem for JCU-NI as they tried to maintain their covert presence in Northern Ireland: there would be nothing covert about being caught on someone else's CCTV entering a premises illegally.

That's where my previous experience with 14th Signal Regiment (Electronic Warfare) gave me an advantage. JCU-NI had a range of military-grade jammers capable of jamming CCTV signals over a wide frequency range. Carried either in a backpack for up-close work, or in a vehicle where a wider range of cameras needed to be knocked out, they were an excellent piece of counter-surveillance kit. Our own cameras worked at a much higher frequency range, thereby ensuring that the jammers didn't interfere.

With the practical side of our training over, we returned to the training building at RAF Aldergrove for a series of training lectures. It would be the first time I would hear the British army's unofficial, insider take on the situation in Northern Ireland, and I was all ears. To my surprise, it wasn't the one-sided propagandist version I was expecting.

The initial lectures covered the civil rights movement and the persecution of the Catholic population that resulted in the first deployment of British troops in August 1969. It also covered, with commendable balance, some of the darkest days in Northern Ireland's history, including criminal acts committed by Loyalist and Republican paramilitaries and by the British army itself. More significantly for me, though, I finally got some insight into the type of unit JCU-NI was.

Charlie, the chief instructor, was the first to speak.

'Most of you have dealt with top-secret information before, but this goes way beyond that. Officially, this unit doesn't exist. The various names, 14 Intelligence Company, FRU or simply "The Det", that you may have heard given to British Intelligence units in Northern Ireland over the years, are all unofficial. The unit is officially the Joint Communications Unit – Northern Ireland or JCU-NI. It consists of nine sub-units called Special Communications Troops or SCTs.

'I am sure that lying around somewhere in the MOD in Whitehall there is a very official description of our mission in Northern Ireland, but I can guarantee you that nowhere does it mention the true nature and objective of this unit. So, in the absence of an official version, I will give you the unofficial version.

'JCU-NI is responsible for the covert surveillance and apprehension of terrorist suspects, both Republican and Loyalist, in support of RUC counter-terrorist operations in Northern Ireland. Note, I said in support of the RUC. We do not share sources and methods with the RUC and we are not a police force. We are here to gather intelligence and where deemed necessary we act on that intelligence, either through the RUC or directly ourselves.

'The unit's emblem, the hundred eyes of the Argus, is precisely what we are: the hidden eyes of British Intelligence in Northern Ireland. We are the watchers. The big difference here is that this Argus has teeth: highly trained operators, not only skilled in covert surveillance but experts in weapons and tactics. This, coupled with attachments of SAS and SBS troopers to each Det, and a dedicated SAS interceptor unit, makes us a highly potent and deadly force.'

I sat there in stunned silence. Can I really be listening to this? I asked myself. I now understood the CO's objections to my being in the unit. It was insane that someone from my background should be privy to information like this. While I had read and heard much about British Intelligence operations in Northern Ireland over the years, this was the first time I had heard it described so matter-of-factly; and by those who had actually carried out many of those operations. I resigned myself to the fact that, as Dave had put it, I really might not be at this unit for too long. The instructor continued.

'Contrary to what the rumour mill might say, the first Det to be established in Northern Ireland was in Derry not Belfast, and so North Det has been given the honour of being called 1 SCT. North Det provides surveillance covering everywhere from Portrush, through Coleraine, Limavady and Derry, down through Strabane and Omagh and finally to the bandit country of East Tyrone and South Armagh. For any of you heading to North Det, bear in mind that their motto is "Train hard, Fight hard, Play hard", and they certainly live up to it.

'2 SCT is based at Moscow camp in the Belfast Docklands and they are responsible for transporting top-secret JCU-NI documents around Northern Ireland [I would later learn that this was not their actual mission]. 3 SCT is based at Palace Barracks in Holywood, Belfast, and they provide surveillance for the entire city of Belfast and surrounding areas. 4 SCT, affectionately known as 'the Arse', is JCU-NI HQ here at Lisburn, providing strategic intelligence and technical and administration support for the outlying operational surveillance Dets.

'5 SCT, 6 SCT, 7 SCT, 8 SCT and 9 SCT are all located in a secure compound at RAF Aldergrove. Between them they are responsible for the southern areas of Fermanagh, Down and South Antrim. They also, through 7 SCT, produce specialist covert imagery systems; in other words, cameras disguised as rocks, trees, et cetera, whatever is needed. While North, East and South Dets all have their own SAS and SBS attachments, there is a permanent dedicated SAS interceptor unit also located at Aldergrove, and when necessary they provide the heavy tactical support to an operation.'

I'm fairly sure my mouth stayed open long after the lecture was over. But it was another lecture that hit the hardest: the story of how two Royal Signals corporals, Derek Wood and David Howes, were killed during their posting at JCU-NI. Like anyone my age, with even the slightest awareness of Northern Ireland, I didn't need to be told the story, but that morning we were given the graphic, no-holds-barred version, and I could feel my stomach tighten and my nerves on edge throughout.

In the darkened room, we were shown the crystal-clear images taken by the specialist camera of an East Det surveillance helicopter that had been covering the funeral of IRA volunteer Kevin Brady on Saturday, 19 March 1988. The funeral cortège was shown moving down the Andersonstown Road in West Belfast towards Milltown cemetery. Sinn Féin stewards were marshalling traffic and providing security in anticipation of another Loyalist attack. Armed PIRA volunteers were mingling with the mourners. The security forces were noticeably absent, giving the area, as it were, a wide birth in an effort to reduce tensions. Three days previously, during the funerals of three IRA volunteers shot dead by British Special forces in Gibraltar, Loyalist gunman Michael Stone had launched a gun and grenade attack at the funerals in Milltown cemetery. Three people had been killed, including Kevin Brady. The events of those two previous weeks had produced some of the tensest moments of the Troubles. Northern Ireland at the time was a powder keg just waiting to explode.

A silver VW Passat was shown approaching the cortège and being stopped by the Sinn Féin stewards and directed to turn around and move away. The vehicle reversed at speed and mounted the pavement. Panic set in among those in the cortège. Was this another Loyalist attack, they must have wondered.

In fact, in the vehicle were Corporal Derek Wood and Corporal David Howes, both members of the British army's Royal Corps of Signals and attached to 2 SCT of JCU-NI. Nonetheless, the vehicle was quickly surrounded, with black taxis either end boxing it in from the front and rear.

As the crowd surrounded the vehicle, Wood drew his pistol and for a few moments the crowd withdrew a little. Wood used this time to try to get out through the window on the driver's side of the car, which had already been smashed in, but the crowd moved in again and began to drag him out of the vehicle.

On the passenger side, the window was smashed and Howes was set upon, though he didn't produce a weapon at any stage. A warning shot was fired into the air by Wood, it was the first and only shot to be fired by either soldier that day. (I had always wondered why they hadn't fired more.)

The crowd forced TV camera crews to stop filming and in some cases confiscated or smashed equipment, although East Det's helicopter kept filming. Both men were eventually dragged to the rear of nearby Casement Park where they were strip-searched and beaten further. A man could now be seen trying to hold back the attackers from the two men as they lay prone, side by side on the ground. He was escorted away though he remained close by. That was Father Alec Reid, a Catholic priest who would go on to be instrumental in the signing of the 1998 Good Friday Agreement.

The men were then thrown over a wall, bundled into taxis and taken a couple of hundred metres away to waste ground near Penny Lane. The beatings and then stabbings continued until both men were eventually shot multiple times at point-blank range. From their arrival on the scene of the funeral, Corporals Wood and Howes were dead in just over twelve minutes.

The television screen went blank and the lights in the room came up. There was a lump in my throat and I swallowed hard to keep down whatever it was. I was sitting in the front row, the only Irishman in the room, – and I could feel the eyes burning into the back of my head. I understood how they must be feeling. It was a deeply uncomfortable moment and for the first time in my British army career I felt ashamed to be Irish.

Thankfully, no one said anything, and the lecture continued.

How this happened from a procedural point of view was the question we needed answered. In the immediate aftermath and for many years thereafter, there was considerable speculation about the two men and why they were in that particular location that day. As always, the MOD had refused to comment and had never clarified what they knew. I only learned the truth that afternoon.

Our second training officer, a huge Welsh man who had spent the previous twenty years as a special duties operator in Northern Ireland, stood at the top of the room and gave us the full story.

'Wood was the "pronto" for 2 SCT. A pronto is the head communications Non-Commissioned Officer (NCO) in a Det. Wood was coming to the end of his current tour in Northern Ireland and was due to rotate back to a normal Royal Corps of Signals unit. Howes was the incoming pronto, just arrived in Northern Ireland and as green as grass as far as working with JCU-NI was concerned.

'Let's be clear: as the head communications operator, a pronto never has call to be on the ground, irrespective of what the rumour mill might have been saying. All his work is based from the operations room at each Det. Routine maintenance, fault repairs and new installations of communications equipment for JCU-NI are carried out by the camera and radio technicians, based in Lisburn. So, while both men were attached to 2 SCT, a covert unit, neither was Special Forces-trained, otherwise the outcome would have been very different that day. For starters, they were nowhere near as armed as a Special Forces operations team would have been, carrying only Browning 9mm pistols.

'More critically, though, they left Moscow camp that morning without checking the "out of bounds" (OOB) board and went on a tour of the city ignorant of what was going on. Wood probably just wanted to show Howes around various JCU-NI locations and maybe a few of the main hot spots too, but this was not part of any official handover procedure. Wood was showboating. Had he checked the board, he would have seen that all of Belfast and most of the rest of Northern Ireland was coded red that day. Even the East Det's own operator teams weren't on the ground. Futhermore, no one from the regular army or 3 SCT knew that Howes and Wood were driving around the city that day.

'Next: when they blundered into the funeral cortège on the Andersonstown Road, they panicked. As the vehicle was surrounded and Wood was being dragged out, he produced his pistol and fired a single warning shot in the air. While his restraint was admirable, it ultimately proved to be fatal. If you look closely at the image on the screen you can see that the magazine housing is empty. Either Wood had been sitting on his pistol for quick access while driving around and accidentally sat on the magazine ejector switch, or it was ejected during the scuffle to get him out of the vehicle. Either way, when he went to fire a second shot all he got was a dead man's click. David Howes never even got to fire a first shot.'

My hand moved under my shirt to my own pistol, still warm from the morning spent on the firing ranges. It was reassuring to have it there.

'As all this was happening, East's helicopter was frantically relaying the vehicle's details back to their operations room based in Palace Barracks. They were convinced that this was another Loyalist attack and, to add to the difficulties, being military, JCU-NI vehicles are not logged on the normal vehicle registration system, but are assigned civilian addresses for security purposes. The car's details were checked on the normal system and came up as a normal civilian vehicle without any flag going up. (At that time there was no central database for JCU-NI vehicles, instead each Det looked after its own.)

'It was a monumental screw-up, yes. But think for a second what might have happened if there'd been a sudden influx of soldiers or police, with armed PIRA members in the crowd. There could have been carnage. I'm not trying to justify what happened or saying that they deserved their fate, but they should never have been there.

'There was no special mission, no clandestine operation, and no cover-up, as has been suggested by some. Howes and Wood were the architects of their own demise. The incident changed forever how special duties and support staff operate here in Northern Ireland and beyond. Many of the drills that you have gone through in the last week of training are a direct result of the deaths of those two men.

'Get this into your heads: you are not Special Forces and if you ever find yourselves in a similar situation, forget all this warning shot bullshit. Shoot first and make it count! It's better to be judged by twelve than carried by six.'

Some years previously, at Blandford camp, I had come across a memorial dedicated to the memory of Howes and Wood. It was an old storage shed hidden away behind the camp gym. I couldn't help wondering, now, if that memorial said more about the British army's attitude towards the two men: ambivalent, at best.

7 THE SHORT STRAW

The compound featured a series of different hangars and buildings, along with two helicopter landing pads. Jason Tech punched in the code on the electronic keypad and as the roller shutter rose we drove in under the watchful eye of several CCTV cameras. My eyes darted around, trying to take it all in. Nothing was in plain sight: all vehicles were tucked away under dustcovers; all windows were blacked out. Dominating it all was a 100-metre-tall mast standing in the middle. It almost seemed to creak under the weight of the antennas and communications dishes hanging from it, which to my trained eye meant there was a hell of a lot going on in this place.

Going about their business were a wide variety of individuals from all walks of life: construction workers, businessmen, housewives and a few who looked like they had spent the night sleeping rough. Not one of them looked like a soldier, though that's precisely what each of them was, in disguise.

The only giveaway that this was a military installation at all, in fact, were the two Gazelle surveillance helicopters on the landing pads.

*

With all the training and modules finished, we three new arrivals sat our final exams. I came out with the highest marks. I was pleased with myself, of course, but had I known what lay ahead as a result, I may well have decided to flunk the whole thing on purpose.

I knocked and entered the OC's office in the HQ building, the first of the three technicians to learn his fate. Bob FoS and Andy Workshops were also present. It was the OC, Richard, who delivered the news.

'Right, Seán, we've given it a lot of thought and based on your previous operational experience and exam results, we think you are the man for North Det.' I stayed silent, giving nothing away, but this wasn't the news I had been hoping for. Richard continued, 'Sorry, Seán, but someone's got to go there and I believe it's only fair that you know exactly what you're heading into. The previous tech, Jason, is returning from North Det after lasting nine months of what should have been a two-year tour. He wants out, but more to the point, North Det want him out. He simply hasn't fitted in and that's why you're replacing him. Your fellow tech will be Alan, a sergeant. He's been there less time than Jason and isn't shaping up too good, either.

'Let me be frank: as it stands, North Det is in pretty dire shape; the operators have no confidence in either their equipment or their technicians. It's reflecting very badly on the Signals Corps but more importantly it's affecting operations. The workload is heavy and we need someone proactive up there. We'll do everything we can to support you from here. The CO expects better from us this time.' I could see Andy Workshops smirking away to himself.

I knew I was being dumped on, but one thing I had learned from my army career to date was that there was no point in moaning about the hand you'd been dealt. After all, they weren't asking me if I wanted to go to North Det, they were ordering me to go. As I stood to leave, I simply said, 'Fair enough. But you know no one has told me exactly what I'll be doing there?' This time it was Andy who chimed in.

'You'll find out when you get there, no sooner. Jason Tech will collect you later today and take you there, and you'll be expected to hit the ground running. Colin Opso, the operations officer, will take some convincing as to your capabilities and perhaps even your loyalties.' Bob FoS raised an eyebrow. I got the distinct impression the decision to send me to North Det had been made as soon as I had arrived … to set me up for a fall.

Well fuck that! I thought, as I left the room to get packed up, I'll show them. I was more determined than ever to earn my place at JCU-NI.

On the journey to North Det, I took the opportunity to question Jason about what it was like, and, to be fair to him, he was completely honest with me. 'I hate the place,' he said, and went on to tell me that the work was unending and technically difficult, and the equipment was nothing like I'd have seen before. 'They expect you to be an expert in every type of kit. It's overwhelming and with only two techs, there's nowhere to hide.' He also confirmed that Colin was a hard taskmaster and expected things done instantly.

He was frank about himself, too. 'I haven't made life easy for myself,' he explained. He admitted to having been pretty lazy with the workload, hoping to be sent back down to 'the Arse'. It worked. North Det was unusual, he went on, in that they do a lot of their own rigging and that means getting out there, on the ground – something Jason wasn't really comfortable with. 'The ops don't like me very much, and they like Alan Tech even less. So don't count on much support from him.'

He described the place as 'the original Big Brother compound: forty of us crammed into a secure compound, 24/7, surrounded by high fences and constantly under CCTV surveillance ourselves. I think they may have based the television show on North Det. No one else enters the compound and we don't mix with anyone from the outside. We are even discouraged from making friends within the unit or learning too much about each other.' He finished by telling me: 'That week off every month that they promised you? Forget about it, it never happens.'

Anything that remained of the picture I had of a great posting was gone. I appreciated Jason's honesty, though, and decided to take on board everything I could from his experience to try to make my own a little easier.

A couple of hours later we arrived at Shackleton Barracks, home of North Det, in the town of Ballykelly, about ten miles from Derry city. The barracks had once been an airfield and so was a vast camp. Tucked away down at the end of the disused airstrip, well away from the rest of the camp, was North Det's compound. The sign outside the compound innocently read 'Royal Signals Special Communications Troop', just as we had been told at our initial briefings. However, the high-security construction of the compound gave a different message: keep well away!

Everyone was headed in the direction of a series of Portakabins, which acted as both the cookhouse and the accommodation block, so Jason and I followed. Unexpectedly, not a single head turned when I entered the cookhouse, at least not until Jason introduced me to Alan. On hearing my accent, heads came up from plates and turned so fast I was surprised that some didn't get whiplash. However, no one said a thing.

Dinner finished, Jason was heading back to Lisburn, his time at North Det over. Sadly, in what amounted to a major deviation from North Det's traditions, there was no leaving party for him. Jason hadn't earned one, it seemed. I just said my thanks and he was gone.

I had decided to start as I meant to go on with Alan Tech; that is, to lead by example despite the fact that he outranked me. So, as I got up from the meal to head for my room, I called across the cookhouse to him: 'See you at 0600 at the tech bay, Alan!' I made sure everyone heard, and sure enough there was a roar of laughter as I walked out. A few minutes later there was a knock at my door and a grinning

Geordie, by the name of Jim, stuck his head in.

'Christ, mate, you know how to make a first impression. Alan hasn't seen 0600 since he was a recruit. Listen, I'm the chief spanner [mechanic] here, so you're stuck with me when it comes to keeping the vehicles on the road. You've got your work cut out here, though, mate. Top tip: if you work hard for Colin, he'll do right by you too.' With that he disappeared, leaving me to ponder how I was going to play things in the following days.

At 0600 the following morning, cup of tea in hand, I met Alan at the tech bay. He was a little bleary-eyed but at least he was there. Our workshop consisted of a double garage, an office and a storeroom packed full of spares. The entire place was in a right mess, equipment lying about all over the place, top-secret documents piled high and a half-stripped vehicle in one of the bays. Before I could tackle any of this, though, I needed to know what exactly my job was. Alan started on a description and fairly soon I felt like I was having an aneurysm.

'We look after the operator vehicle fit-outs, specialist sur-veillance vehicle fit-outs, operator-body communications, covert-camera installations, radio communications and anything else that Colin decides to throw at us. We have over twenty operator vehicles, twelve specialist vehicles, two covert-surveillance motorbikes, eighteen operators, approximately twenty overt-surveillance cameras and who knows how many covert cameras. Oh, and because no one else is allowed on to the compound, we look after the phones and Sky TV, too.' Alan was grinning from ear to ear while delivering this summary, and so despite it all I couldn't help but laugh. At first I found the nature of what we did difficult to believe, it was all so very 007. But three years and almost a hundred vehicle fit-outs later, I was taking it for granted.

A covert-operator vehicle fit-out involves installing a hell of a lot of equipment, which means the vehicle has to be completely stripped out. For example, the communications system includes an induction loop hidden in the roof lining of the vehicle, allowing the operator to communicate through the covert microphone hidden in the sun visor and his covert earpiece. The earpiece was not one of those used by other agencies with the ridiculous curly cord attached but a high-tech wireless device that was almost invisible to the naked eye. On top of that, the gear stick is fitted with a covert switch to enable the operator to control when he transmits.

One of the telltale signs of other 'undercover' vehicles is the number of communications antennas fitted to them. Not so at North Det, where a single, specially designed, encrypted version allowed the covert communications system, in-car entertainment system and the covert video-camera signals all to be broadcast from one standard-looking antenna that matched each individual vehicle perfectly.

There was a whole range of locations in a vehicle where covert video cameras could be hidden: from the rear-view mirror to the headrests, from the boot (looking through specially made opaque number plates, for example) to those hidden in loose items left lying around inside the vehicle. Most of these cameras had pan, tilt and zoom functions and could be either recorded within the vehicle itself or broadcast back to the operations room for live viewing. There were also stills cameras hidden in various locations in each vehicle, controlled by a switch located close to the driver's seat. These were used for taking identification shots of suspects.

Since the Howes and Wood murders in 1988, all operator vehicles were fitted with what were known as 'perks plates' (plastic-explosive reactive plates), small disk-like plates about the size of a saucer that were attached to the underside of the vehicle on both the driver and passenger sides. The plates were packed with a small amount of explosives and ball bearings. Hidden on the dashboard of each vehicle, then, was an arm and fire switch. When operated, the plates would fire, driving anyone who surrounded the vehicle away and giving the driver a better chance to escape a dangerous situation. Also fitted to the vehicles was a covert alarm system, known as 'hardtac' (a hard-wired tactical alarm). While silent within the vehicle itself, this system would broadcast over the radio net back to the operations room, alerting everyone to the fact that a vehicle had been compromised.

One of the most difficult pieces of equipment to fit was the search gear. It was a nightmare job that all technicians hated. The kit allowed the operators to track weapons, vehicles or 'targets' that had tracking devices fitted to them. The antenna was covertly fitted into the sun visor and an audio-visual display was fitted to the dashboard, giving the operator a clear indication of when he was getting closer to a device. It also had one further and very important function: each operator wore a specially designed wristwatch, which – when the outer bevel was turned to a pre-determined number on the dial – acted as a tracking device. If any of the operators was ever snatched, the Det could track them instantly to their location.

Up to speed on what type of work I would be doing, it was time to meet everyone and first up was Colin, our operations officer. As I entered the operations building, I noticed a couple of things that I would later learn were down to a lack of trust in me at the beginning. Throughout the reception area, operations room and 'spooks bay' were a series of bulletin boards that displayed photos of, addresses of, known associates of, vehicle registrations belonging to and other information on, North Det's main targets. Each one was covered by a blackout roller blind every time I entered the building (something I was never encouraged to do during my first month or so). Another example was how the encryption device for the radio communications was changed every week and stored in a cabinet in the communications room; that was locked anytime I was around. I didn't take any offence, though; in fact, I was constantly surprised that I was anywhere near this stuff myself.

Colin was waiting for me, alone in the operations room. He was a middle-aged man from Manchester and scruffy as hell. He had spent most of his JCU-NI career at North Det, first as an operator and now as an Opso.

'Right, Seán, the last two techs they sent me were shit and I'm not expecting too much more from you. I hope you prove me wrong. I don't care where you're from but until you prove to me that you're capable, you're on a short leash. I don't know how bad a state the vehicles are in but we can barely get communications from them in Derry, never mind down into the border areas. I want a full assessment as a priority. I need to know how bad things really are. I have a feeling that you're going to have to refit every vehicle we have. I think the stores are full of covert cameras that have never been deployed. I want those shelves cleared and those cameras fitted to the ops vehicles. Just so you understand: there is no limit to the budget here, so whatever you need, you'll get. Alan Tech is a lazy bastard but a likeable lazy bastard and that's the only reason he's still here. And just so you know, we have a new intake of operators arriving in about six weeks and they'll all need new vehicles fitted out, too.'

This was worse than I thought and maybe getting returned from North Det might not be the worst thing that could happen to me. Colin must have been reading my mind.

'I make no apologies for the workload, Seán, but it is rewarding when we get it right. How well do you know your way around Northern Ireland?'

'Well enough, I suppose,' I replied, smiling at the question. Colin smiled back.

'I thought you might. Could come in handy down the line.'

I spent the rest of the day going around introducing myself to everyone. I soon learned that the Det spoke a different language. Everyone was referred to by their first name followed by their job description, so I was now Seán Tech. It was as much a security measure as an ease of remembering people's names and roles. It also prevented confusion when two people on the Det had the same name. I met Ali DQ, the Det quartermaster, in supplies, where I put in an order for a lengthy list of equipment. From there I was introduced to the intelligence officers, known as spooks, who informed me that I would have a security vetting meeting with 'the Ferret' the following day. It turned out to be nothing more than a chat to ask if I had any secrets I would like to reveal to him; things like gambling debts or that I was a homosexual; anything that could be used against me by the enemy. Next was Will, the photographer on the Det, known as 'the brownie', followed by Jamie Pronto and 'the eight bleeps' – slang for the Royal Signals communications operators who manned the radio network. I caught up with Jim Spanner and met Paul Spanner, the mechanics with whom I would work very closely over the next few years. At lunch I was introduced to the two chefs who looked after us all.

Last but not least, I met Simon OC of North Det, and the rest of the operators. This included the two SAS lads, known as 'sugars' and the two SBS lads, known as 'shakeys'. They were all gathered in the briefing room and when I entered, Colin introduced me. I wasn't quite sure how to approach this so I decided on a bit of humour.

'I'm not planning on being here too long. Apparently, I'm

meeting someone called "the Ferret" tomorrow so that should put an end to it. With that in mind, if you could all write down your names and addresses for me, I'll pass them on to Gerry and Martin as soon as I get over the border.'

Much to my relief, the room erupted with laughter and calls to 'water-board him!' and suchlike. I had struck the right note. It didn't stop them hitting me with complaints about their vehicles and the faults they were experiencing, however!

Overall, I realised, there were two ways of responding to the challenge: either collapse under the enormity of it and prove Andy Workshops right or buckle down and prove everyone wrong. I chose the latter. At least if I failed I could say I gave it my best shot.

After dinner that evening everyone went to the bar, myself included. Covering the walls were photographs and newspaper cuttings documenting North Det's successes since its first inception. I stopped at one framed collage and stood in shock, dizzy from inner conflict. It was newspaper cuttings and celebratory photographs of the ambush of the IRA unit at Loughgall from May 1987, the one at which my aunt's cousin, Seamus Donnelly, was killed. You could have knocked me over with a feather, and I didn't notice Colin coming up behind me.

'One of our better results that, Seán,' he said. 'I told you: when North gets it right, we really get it right. The SAS lads might have gotten the credit for the dirty work but it was us who did all the surveillance for it.'

Despite all the training and briefings and insights of the previous month, it was only at this moment that the proverbial penny dropped finally as to what I was really doing here – working for a covert British army unit in my own country.

8 FIRST OPERATION

The first month was difficult in terms of both the workload I had and the fact that I wasn't fully accepted as part of the team. A test of both was just what I needed.

*

It all started in early February 2002, when the heads of departments were summoned to the briefing room at North Det's covert compound in Ballykelly. A group of PSNI (Police Service of Northern Ireland) officers were among those who attended the briefing. I would later learn that these were members of the PSNI's Tasking and Co-ordination Group (TCG) (later to be renamed Regional Coordinating Group). Apparently, an attack on an PSNI patrol in Coalisland using an RPG 22 rocket launcher was imminent. The Soviet-designed weapon had an effective range of 160m and could penetrate steel armour as thick as 400mm: a truly potent weapon.

The surveillance operation being mounted by North Det that week was aimed at apprehending the four men while they were in possession of that rocket launcher. The TCG would be positioned and ready to move in so that at the trial it could be presented as if PSNI officers had carried out the surveillance and made the arrests.

Such details were not revealed to me at that stage. I was too green, in both senses of the word: I had only just joined North Det, and I was a Southerner who had yet to prove that I could be trusted. Although most at North Det were friendly enough towards me in that first month, there was still an air of suspicion over my appointment. They didn't like outsiders at the best of times and being from the Republic made my fitting in all the more difficult. Besides, I was still getting to grips with what exactly went on at this highly secretive unit and busy working my way through the backlog of technical faults that had built up.

I knew something was up. Alan arrived back to our tech bay following the briefing and informed me that Colin wanted to see me in his office. With Alan unable to provide any more information, I made my way across the compound, a little concerned about what lay ahead. Might I already be on my way out?

On the contrary, Colin was direct and to the point: 'What condition is the Det in technically at this point, Seán?' A simple question, yes, but at the same time tricky for me. I had to choose between telling the truth, thereby putting the spotlight on Alan, and lying, potentially putting the operation at risk. Under a calm exterior I was panicking. 'Well?' Colin pressed. He wasn't known for his patience. At any other unit I probably would have waffled for a bit and hoped to avoid committing one way or another, but I got the impression that there was no place for bullshit here.

'Sorry,' I began, 'but given the current state of the vehicles, I can't guarantee full communications or video-surveillance coverage anywhere within our AOR [Area of Responsibility].' This was seriously bad news to deliver to any operations officer, and I waited for the explosion that I was sure would follow. In fact, Colin just nodded and fired another question at me: 'What do you know about the situation in Coalisland and the surrounding area?' I quickly tried to recall details from my initial radio and cameras training at Lisburn a couple of months earlier.

'Communications down there are sketchy at best,' I replied more quickly, 'and at worst non-existent. Camera coverage would depend on what you want to achieve, and where. I can't guarantee full video surveillance or radio coverage that close to the border. Coalisland is a notorious dead spot.' It was a terrible generalisation but the best I could do under the circumstances.

'Okay. Put a plan together, Seán, and be back here in an hour with whatever gear you need. You're forward-mounting to Dungannon RUC station. Your call sign is Tuner.'

I left the ops building in some kind of shock and none the wiser about the actual operation. Talk about a baptism of fire, I thought to myself. Was it a test? Damn right it was! But also my chance to put down a marker and prove that I deserved to be here.

An hour later, sweating, I pulled up outside the ops building in an old Ford Transit van. On the exterior it looked just like any old decorator's van, giving the impression of being full of old sheets, paint tins and a ladder or two. Not so, however. This one was made entirely of fibreglass to allow its signal booster (what we called a 'high power') to operate from within, unhindered by metal. Placing the vehicle within the target area in Coalisland, I reckoned, would allow the operator's radio signals to be picked up by the high power, transmitted back to the communications mast in Dungannon and then boosted on to the ops room at Ballykelly, and vice versa. Or at least, so I hoped. My instruction to get the video surveillance from the covert cameras back to the Det would have to wait until I got to Dungannon.

I went straight to the armoury and withdrew my SIG sauer 9mm pistol, three clips of ammunition and a HK53 assault rifle pre-loaded with two magazines. Meanwhile, the operators were deploying to Coalisland en masse. They were in a variety of civilian-looking vehicles but the true nature of these vehicles was hidden. They were fitted with everything from armoured doors and seats to covert communications, video-surveillance kit and explosive plates on the undercarriage. Not one of the operators looked in the least bit like a soldier, dressed instead to blend in with the general population as much as possible, and they went to extraordinary lengths to do so. All the vehicles had their number plates changed that morning to reflect the area we were operating in, my vehicle included.

I left in the middle of the pack of operators heading for Dungannon to get some protection front and back in case I stumbled upon any trouble. Illegal paramilitary checkpoints (IVCPs) were not uncommon, especially down in bandit country, close to the border. Despite being armed myself and sandwiched by the operators, I was scared shitless. I knew very little happened in these parts without the local population taking notice, and while all the operators were trained for things like their cover being blown, I wasn't.

With my own earpiece fitted, I listened to the operators' radio checks as they moved towards Coalisland. It was a completely different language they were speaking. Instead of naming locations, they used different colours and numbers: 'Going through Red 15 toward Red 16', etc. As for me, I simply made my way from memory down through Strabane, Newtownstewart and Omagh. Worryingly, the closer we got to Coalisland, the worse the communications got. As contact with the ops room broke up, the operators were going nuts. There were more than a few 'fucking techs' being bandied about over the radio network, making me even more anxious.

As we neared Dungannon, the operators broke off and went about setting up their own surveillance net, directed by Colin Opso from Ballykelly. I pulled up outside the PSNI station and the gates opened immediately. Thanks to the TCG, they were expecting both me and the vehicle. I had no sooner unloaded my kit into the communications hut at the base of a large mast than Colin Opso came on the radio net.

'Tuner, this is Alpha, get a move on!' I got the high power ready in the back of the Ford and put a call through to Lee Op, an operator from the Parachute Regiment, to come and pick it up. He arrived shortly afterwards and I briefed him on how to operate and where best to place the device.

'I hope for your sake this thing works. The lads are having a nightmare on the ground with the radios. Colin has dropped you right in it!' he said, grinning as he pulled away. Twenty minutes later, sure enough, he was back, having inserted the vehicle and been picked up by Big Rick, one of the SAS troopers attached to North Det. Unbearably, it would be at least another hour of sweating it before the operators had finished their testing for dead spots and I could find out if everything worked.

The call finally came over the net that communications were 'Lima Charlie' – loud and clear. First hurdle over, I could breathe a sigh of relief. Only one, though: I had two covert cameras to sort out. My hut was freezing cold and full of North Det equipment, but I had been warned by Colin to keep away from the PSNI station itself and, even more importantly, to keep the PSNI well away from our kit. I got the sense that there wasn't much trust there.

The observation post, with two surveillance cameras, was to be established in the field adjacent to Loughview Road. Big Rick and Gerry Op, an SBS sergeant, would be manning the observation post. They would remain in there until the conclusion of the operation. I had two high-powered surveillance cameras with me, each capable of zooming in on a vehicle number plate from half a kilometre away. This would allow Colin to focus in on any details he wanted. Both cameras could be switched from day to night mode, eliminating any problem with the cover that darkness might be assumed to provide.

The cameras would be powered by M1, military-grade batteries made specifically for covert observation posts. They could power a hidden camera for months without needing to be charged: crucial when trying to maintain the secret nature of a surveillance post. Getting the cameras into position was the operators' problem and would begin at about midnight that night. Getting the images back to Colin at the operations room was mine. Both Coalisland and Dungannon had overt-surveillance cameras positioned on local masts, their feeds travelling via a heavily encrypted and highly sophisticated fibre-optic network. My plan was to piggy-back the images from my two covert cameras on that overt camera feed, allowing Colin to switch between them. I set up a test run within the compound, beaming the images the few feet from the hut to the mast then back to Ballykelly. It worked. Whether it would work once buried in a field four miles away was another matter.

Big Rick and Gerry arrived about 2200 hours that night and I went through how to set up and test the cameras. It was after midnight before Lee arrived to collect them and their gear. By now, both were dressed in camouflaged sniper suits and had all the equipment and weapons they would need while in the observation post. It was the first time I had seen either looking like a true soldier but it was nothing new for them: this was the type of work that SAS and SBS troopers had been trained for.

They piled into the back of the van and set off. When I got back to listen in to the radio communications, all chatter on the network had stopped. Only a series of clicks and beeps confirmed the position of the men now. Lee made his way down Loughview Road, pausing for the briefest moment to allow Big Rick and Gerry to alight. All the while the other operators were providing a surveillance cordon, ensuring that no one was observing the drop-off. Big Rick and Gerry made their way silently through the undergrowth to the prearranged position for the observation post. It took about twenty minutes to get settled in and ensure they would be out of sight even in daylight. They then began positioning the two covert cameras.

The first one worked like a dream, the image arriving at Dungannon and Ballykelly without a hitch. I was thrilled. The lads moved further up the tree line to position the second camera. I was devastated when I heard Colin on the network to Gerry: 'No image here.' They went through the set-up procedure again. Still nothing. 'Tuner, what's going on down there?' I heard Colin growling down the net at me. I was busy going through my own fault-finding procedure in my head. There was only one thing that I could think of, and Big Rick and Gerry wouldn't like it.

'November, this is Tuner. Can you check that the camera is switched on?' Seconds later the image popped up on my screen and Colin 's simultaneously.

'Nice one, Tuner,' I heard Colin say.

The week that followed was a nightmare for me as I had to fix an avalanche of faults with the operators' equipment, all under serious pressure. I alternated between sleep and listening in as the operators followed the four men around the surrounding area. I was amazed at how closely the four were being monitored, literally every minute of the day, with nothing left to chance. Every person the targets came in contact with was photographed using either covert stills or video cameras fitted to the operators' vehicles and then run through the British Intelligence database. If they weren't yet in the database, they were added – potential new targets for North Det.

Finally, the time came. The targets had been tailed to Loughview Road and had suddenly entered the field. 'Standby! Standby!' rang out over the net. It was Big Rick and Gerry in the observation post. Time seemed to stand still. Eventually, three of the targets moved across the field, having collected the RPG 22. It was unclear if the men had any other weapons on them. It wouldn't matter as there was enough firepower between the North Det operators to make it a very one-sided fight. The sense of anticipation was intense.

Next, Colin gave the order and the TCG moved in. Despite an attempt to run away, all three men were detained without a fight. Each was found to be wearing gloves, two carrying the rocket launcher and one a pair of bolt cutters. The fourth man was arrested in a nearby car park, a can of petrol stuffed with a rag on the ground behind the car he was sitting in, presumably to torch the vehicle after the attack.

What impressed me most was how rapidly and inconspicuously all North Det personnel withdrew from the area. Big Rick and Gerry were picked up by Lee and everyone was on the way back to Ballykelly within fifteen minutes. They simply disappeared from the scene as if they had never even been there. I got a clear sense of how these guys were the hidden eyes and ears of British Intelligence.

I packed up my own gear and drove the van back to Ballykelly, operators overtaking me on the way. As the adrenaline faded and the lack of sleep soon took its toll, I suddenly realised just how exhausted I was by the whole experience. As the roller shutter went up at North's secure compound, I could hear the celebrations already beginning. They would last for two days, I was told, with everyone letting off steam in a big way. As tradition dictated, each of the other Dets had sent a barrel of beer to mark North Det's success.

I needed some sleep first, but as I made my way across to the Portakabin that served as my room, I heard a shout: 'Seán! Bar! Now!' It was Colin. As I entered, he walked over and handed me a beer. 'You'll do,' he said.

Despite the apparent success of the operation, all four

men would later be acquitted of Real IRA membership, of conspiring to murder and of possession of an RPG rocket launcher. The reasons given by the trial judge pointed to unexplained references during the trial to military personnel not included in PSNI notes on the arrests, and a failure to disclose briefings received by the PSNI from the military. There was also a lack of specific forensic evidence linking the men to the rocket launcher.

The problem was: the Det didn't exist officially and so no legal reference could ever be made to it. Its covert nature was its strength in operations but would sometimes prove a major hindrance in prosecutions.

9 HARE & HOUNDS

After my contribution to the operation at Coalisland, the attitude of Colin Opso and the rest towards me changed. And it changed completely. Suddenly I was allowed to come and go as I pleased. I took my place at the appropriate briefings and was privy to some of the most sensitive information available to British Intelligence in Northern Ireland. I was now one of the North Det team.

But there was another factor that still distinguished me from the other technicians and, I think, most of the other soldiers who served at the Dets in Northern Ireland: I had a deep personal interest in what was going on. My fascination was not just with the players and the operations and their deadly cat and mouse games played out every day with the paramilitaries, though I wouldn't deny I loved all that. I was also curious about the people and their backgrounds and their attitudes towards what was going on.

At the first opportunity, I hooked up my own Cougar radio. I tuned to the JCU-NI radio network to a speaker in the tech bay, primarily to keep tabs on any problems that the operators were having with their vehicles, but also to satisfy my own curiosity; to listen in from this angle on my country's ongoing struggle with its past. I learned a huge amount about both British Intelligence and about the ever-expanding paramilitary organisations in Northern Ireland, most of which both surprised and disappointed me. I also learned a whole lot about myself and the attitudes towards the North that I

had been carrying with me since childhood.
 Things were changing.   ✱

My first few months at North Det flew by. I didn't leave the compound for a single minute, other than for training courses, such was the workload. At least I had the scope of the backlog figured out and was making some headway. The trouble was that every time I started to get some momentum built up, I would be lumbered with yet another task. For instance, after a couple of months I discovered that it was my job to carry out all the counter-surveillance sweeps at the Det. They realised I had the necessary training and I became the go-to man for technical surveillance counter-measures (TSCM). Every week I would sweep the operations and briefing rooms, and after every meeting attended by the PSNI TCG, I would sweep all the buildings.

The TCG was a necessary part of operating in Northern Ireland. They not only carried out any arrests that the Det identified but they also ensured that during ops no friendly fire or hassle came our way from the rest of the PSNI. That being said, they were never fully trusted in JCU-NI circles. Just as it had been for me at the beginning of my stint, all information boards, equipment and the CCTV monitor wall that dominated the operations room were covered when TCG were around. They were allowed into the briefing room and nowhere else.

I was buried in catch-up work one day when the encrypted telephone unit on my desk rang. I swore silently to myself at the interruption. It was Jamie Pronto from the ops room to say that Jim Spanner and myself were wanted in the briefing room to meet the new ops. We were met by Colin and six male operators, all on their first tour with the Det. As well as it being a policy that no Det postings were to know each other from before, all operators also changed their names for such a posting. If they were ever snatched, they could never reveal much of use about the other operators. In this batch, there was Kevin Op and Damien Op, both 'sugars'. Damien was a hard-ass Kiwi who had transferred from the New Zealand SAS to the British SAS. There was Baz Op, a good-natured cockney, and Fred Op both from infantry units. There was Brian Op from the Royal Engineers and, finally, Stephen Op, a 'shakey' trooper. All of them seemed to me to be decent guys – not always the case at North Det.

It was down to Jim and me to match the vehicle to the operator and it had to be believable. Just as a young hipster guy didn't drive around in a brand-new Audi, a successful, well-groomed businessman didn't own a clapped-out Citroën. We looked the six of them over and came to the same conclusion: they all looked the bloody same! In trying so hard not to look like soldiers, they now, in fact, stood out as stereotypical young, scruffy louts. The many young men who looked after themselves, who spruced themselves up and wore trendy clothes, were not represented here at all. Jim told Colin they'd need to mix up their appearances a bit before we ordered the vehicles. Colin knew this already, of course, but always welcomed other people's input. A few haircuts, shaves and wardrobe makeovers later, Jim had the new vehicles in place, ready for their covert fit-outs.

Det selection was open to all members of the British armed services and, so as to offer the Opso a wider variety of scenarios on the ground, women were positively encouraged to try for selection. Every operator underwent six months' rigorous training prior to arriving at their Det. They were trained at a facility close to the SAS HQ at Hereford and the training was physically and mentally tough. Working alone and in difficult circumstances required great stamina and mental strength, both of which were tested to breaking point. As part of that, the operators were given advanced driving lessons, including sustained high-speed driving, using a vehicle as a weapon, controlled crashing, J-turns, skid recovery and anti-ambush drills. Once they arrived at the Det and received their own vehicle, they were encouraged to go out on to the airfield and practise it all again, since every vehicle handles differently, especially once all its armour and equipment is fitted.

Photographic and video surveillance was a large part of Det surveillance and the operators were taught advanced photography and video skills. They chose for themselves where they wanted their cameras to be fitted in their vehicles, though sometimes their suggestions weren't the most practical.

Covert surveillance involves a wide variety of scenarios, ranging from rural surveillance out of ditches or hides, to following a suspect through built-up areas on foot or in a vehicle, to what was officially labelled 'covert methods of entry'(CMOE): burglary to you and me. The operators were taught to pick locks, make duplicate keys, break into vehicles and neutralise security systems. Each Det had a CMOE cell, which was a closely guarded secret. Planting listening devices was another aspect of their work: breaking into a premises and planting a device was easy, they were told; doing it without anyone knowing you've been there was the real skill. The operators were trained in close-quarters combat, unarmed combat and in handling a wide variety of weapons, including SIG sauer 9mm and Walther PPK pistols, HK MP5 sub-machine guns, HK 53 assault rifles and all manner of shotguns.

Despite all this training, the operators still weren't fully ready for action when they arrived. Once on-site, they had six weeks to become familiar with their areas and all the relevant information about them. This was actually the most difficult aspect of the preparation for many, involving so much memorising and unfamiliar names, but failure to master it would see them sent back for further training or, even, returned to their parent unit.

Of course, no operator, no matter how good, could learn every street and road within their AOR off by heart, so a navigation system, known as 'the spots', was designed to make this information easier to learn and more secure. Every area was designated a colour (for instance, the Bogside could be called 'Red') and every road junction, roundabout exit and street within an area was given a number. So you could have an operator calling over the net, 'Heading from Red 16 to Red 17'. Back at the Det, a large map showing all the colour spots and numbers was used to track each operator and report on the movements of targets. (Colin also used Scrabble tiles to give himself a full picture of where all his operators were at any given time, and he moved them around the map as and when required.)

Though it took some learning at the start, it was a very simple system and very secure. In the highly unlikely event of the encryption on the radios being compromised, anyone listening in would have no idea what the operators were on about. With the radio network on at all times in the tech bay, after my time at North Det, I knew 'the spots' as well as I knew the actual place names.

The best training exercise at North Det was called 'hare & hounds', and each of the new arrivals was put through it time and again until they had everything they needed to know about the area committed to memory. It also tested their counter-surveillance skills.

Something that is often forgotten in surveillance work is that sometimes the hunter becomes the hunted. The paramilitaries, in particular PIRA members, were quite adept at counter-surveillance and in the right circumstances were more than capable of picking out an operator, especially if the operator became sloppy. They had a network of lookouts of their own posted around their neighbourhoods, usually young males, looking for the telltale signs that they might be under surveillance. Once spotted, an operator was likely to find themselves the subject of surveillance and so had to know how to shake it off.

The exercise was simple: a lead car, the hare, would be sent off from Ballykelly at first light with a thirty-minute head start. They could travel anywhere within North Det's zone, and after thirty minutes the rest of the surveillance team, the hounds, would be sent in pursuit. Guided from the operations room, using the overt CCTV cameras, the hounds would try to locate and track, unnoticed, the hare.

Early one morning, not long into the new ops training period, the one called Damien Op knocked at my office door.

'Colin says to grab your weapon and ride along with me for hare & hounds this morning.' I was more than a little surprised and called Colin.

'It looks like you're going to be with us for a while,' he explained, 'so you might as well get to know "the ground" and the problems the guys are facing with the kit. Besides, you deserve a day off.' I could sense he was smiling away to himself. 'Just don't drop yourself or Damien Op in the shit!' he barked before hanging up.

Amazing, I thought to myself, a few weeks ago I was under a cloud of suspicion and here I was heading out on the ground with an SAS trooper! I grabbed my pistol from the armoury, attached my pager and spare magazines to my belt, and jumped into Damien's vehicle. As we left the compound, we both inserted our covert earpieces and did our radio checks back to the operations room. That would be the only check until the exercise was over.

Thirty minutes of road later we heard on the net the words 'Hounds are released', and knew we were now being hunted. As he drove around Derry city, Damien started to point out some of the main players on North Det's target list, more for his own benefit than mine, I soon realised. Despite what many may think, there were within North Det's area of operations fewer than thirty active members in the IRA, meaning those who actually went out and did the shootings or planted the bombs. While there was a considerable support network, and even more armchair Republicans, the foot soldiers were few and far between.

Many on the list meant nothing to me but I instantly recognised Willie McGuinness, brother of Martin McGuinness, and suspected OC of Derry PIRA; and the two prominent Sinn Féin councillors, Raymond and Andrew McCartney, who would later prove to be a major thorn in North Det's side. We drove passed Harvey Street, North Det's number one target location, and from there we passed one of the favourite drinking dens of the lower-ranked members of the IRA, the Bogside Inn. (None of the important players were mad enough ever be on display in such a high-profile location.) We passed the home of a suspected but, as yet, unconfirmed informer for British Intelligence. (He would later have a large influence on North Det operations.) From Derry, we made our way down to Strabane and Omagh, through some of the most staunchly Republican areas in Northern Ireland.

Our trail was eventually picked up by the hounds.

Rural surveillance is very difficult to maintain, what with open stretches of road and little or no cover available from other traffic. That is where North Det's surveillance helicopter would come in. Each Gazelle helicopter carried sophisticated video-surveillance equipment, forward looking infra-red (FLIR) cameras and search equipment that can track planted devices. A Det operator would be the passenger in the helicopter while it was flown at the right height to go unnoticed on the ground but still able to provide a visual on the target.

Damien's plan was to first lose the tail cars on the back roads between Omagh and Derry and then shake off the helicopter in the streets of the city. It sounded good to me. As we drove along the narrow roads at breakneck speed, he would occasionally stop to allow any vehicles behind him to pass, making note of each model and registration before moving on.

While the new operators struggled a little to go unnoticed in the rural areas (though by the end of their six weeks they would have it mastered), in the built-up areas of Derry city, Omagh and Strabane, they did much better. Even when Damien and I went on foot and darted in and out of shops and down side streets, they still managed to keep up surveillance without either of us spotting them. Considering we knew who we were looking for, that was no mean feat. I was impressed.

The six-week familiarisation period was soon up and the newbies were to hear of their fate. There was usually a little bet between the other North Det members on who might fail, but on this occasion there was no point. Everyone knew the group had done well but that Brian Op would be leaving anyhow. It wasn't that he hadn't got to grips with the job, in fact the opposite: he was better than some of the others; it was just that he had got on the wrong side of Colin and that meant he was doomed.

On the final evening, the six arrived back in their vehicles and headed straight for the debriefing room. An hour or so later, they re-emerged. Kevin, Damien, Baz, Fred and Stephen headed straight over to the bar to begin celebrating, while Brian headed to his room to pack up and leave. He was taken by helicopter to Lisburn and was soon on a flight back to the UK. I never saw him again. It was definitely a shame that we lost such a good operator, but Colin didn't need any reason to sack someone other than that they didn't fit in. I could see clearly that although Simon OC was in charge on paper, in practice Colin had the last word at the Det.

That night in the bar we drank until the small hours. A replica painting of the Free Derry wall was at one end of the bar and when anyone would finish a bottle of beer, the bottle would be thrown and smashed against the painting: another one of North Det's bizarre traditions.

Over the next few years I built a strong bond with those five new operators. In spite of the rules about friendship, many Det members did become friends. We took trips together, including across the border into the Republic. Despite the strict rules around learning personal information about each other, we did learn some of each other's real names. In some cases we even became familiar with each other's backgrounds. More importantly we kept each other going through the often long and boring phases of life at North Det.

10 THE COLOMBIAN CONNECTION

The trouble with always being armed is that you became so comfortable with carrying a concealed weapon you sometimes forget you have it on you at all.

*

I walked towards the X-ray scanner and metal-detector security point at Belfast International Airport when something suddenly put my heart crossways in me: I still had my pistol tucked into my waistband and the spare magazines still clipped to my belt.

I stopped dead in my tracks and turned to walk away. This immediately caught the attention of the armed officer on duty, of course.

'Excuse me, sir!' he called after me. 'Stay where you are, please!' I cringed but stopped and turned back to face him. He walked over to meet me, hand covering the trigger guard of his Heckler & Koch sub-machine gun. Undoubtedly by now his trained eye could make out the two bulges concealed under my loose-fitting jersey. Upon request I slowly opened my wallet and discreetly showed my military ID card. 'Forgot you were carrying, did you?' he asked with a smile. 'On your way, so. Just try remember in future, mate.' I left the airport rather sheepishly, silently cursing North Det operator, Sharon, since she was the reason I was there in the first place.

Five minutes later, Sharon herself popped the boot, threw in her bags and jumped into the passenger seat beside me.

She and three of the other operators had been absent from the Det for about two months now, apparently for a training exercise back in the UK. As I handed her her pistol, I asked casually but with a noticeable smile: 'So how was Colombia, Shar?'

'You're not supposed to know about that, Seán,' she answered, smiling back.

There are very few secrets at North Det but the deployment of personnel and equipment to Colombia had to be one of the worst-kept secrets in its history. Besides, her tan was so deep that she could have passed for a Colombian herself. As we made the long and boring journey from the airport back to Ballykelly, I got the full story, much of which I had already pieced together myself from the strange goings-on in the previous months back at base. The operation had ruffled more than a few feathers at JCU-NI and had caused me more than a few headaches as well.

It all started in August 2001 when three Irishmen, travelling under false passports, were arrested in Bogota airport by the Colombian intelligence service, acting on a tip off. Their flight had come from San Vicente del Caguán, the largest town in a region controlled by the Marxist guerrilla army group, the Revolutionary Armed Forces of Colombia ('FARC'). The three men – James Monaghan, Martin McCauley and Niall Connolly – were suspected of having spent the previous five weeks teaching FARC guerrillas how to produce mortars and IEDs, and training them in the use of weapons. All three had connecting flights out of Colombia; Monaghan and McCauley were heading for Belfast via Paris, and Connolly was bound for Dublin via Caracas and Madrid. Those journeys were now halted and their arrest was soon international news. All three men were well known to British Intelligence, in particular Monaghan and McCauley. In fact, it was believed that British Intelligence had supplied the tip-off to the Colombians in the first place.

Originally from Donegal, James Monaghan was a prominent Republican figure and convicted terrorist. He was credited with developing the IRA's first mortar bomb back in the early 1970s, along with the later replacement of devices requiring command wires with remote control devices. Martin McCauley was born in Armagh and had a two-year suspended sentence for possession of weapons to his name and was considered by many at North Det to be one of the IRA's best engineers. Niall Connolly was born in Glenageary, Co. Dublin, and educated at Trinity College, Dublin. He was the only one of the three who was a fluent Spanish speaker, and he had extensive experience in South America, having worked there for a number of years. Prior to his arrest, he was living in Cuba, where he was a representative for Sinn Féin. This was initially denied by the party, but they later confirmed that he had been working in Cuba as a Sinn Féin representative.

It had long been suspected within JCU-NI circles that the IRA had made contact with FARC, but now it was confirmed and in the public domain. It was also suspected that the three men arrested in Bogota weren't the first IRA members to travel to Colombia to meet with FARC. FARC had, under the command of Manuel Marulanda (known as Tirofijo, meaning 'sure shot'), been fighting the government from the jungles of Colombia for decades, but now planned to bring their campaign into the urban centres. To do this they needed to be schooled in the art of urban guerilla warfare, and that's where the IRA came in. The deal between FARC and the IRA was thought to be a very lucrative one for the IRA. They would, through the likes of Monaghan and McCauley, provide expertise and training in return for millions in cash, something FARC had in abundance from the illegal trade in cocaine.

Even worse, the new dissident Republican groups were

now known to be moving into the drugs trade. With the possibility of a regular and cheap supply of cocaine coming into their possession from FARC, it didn't bode well for either the people of Northern Ireland or the security forces. Infighting over drug territories had caused havoc within the Loyalist paramilitary groups and it was something the security forces in Northern Ireland were keen not to see spreading to the Republicans. A huge influx of cash into the Republican movement at a time when so many splinter groups were popping up could start a new and prolonged phase of the Troubles. British Intelligence services made the decision (eight months after the initial arrest of the three Irishmen, which seems slow) to step in and provide their own support to the Colombian government and they decided to do this through JCU-NI. And because Monaghan and McCauley had operated within North Det's area of responsibility (both had previously had Charlie One status there), it fell to us to take on the Colombian operation.

Rosetta Stone must have made a fortune from North Det in May/June of 2002 because everyone seemed to be plugged into beginner's Spanish lessons. There was only a limited number of spots for the Colombia operation and the operators were competing against one another to make the cut. This was all causing a major distraction from day-to-day surveillance operations. Some operators were spending more time listening to Spanish CDs in their cars than to the radio net. The whole thing was making Colin very unhappy. Things were about to get worse, too, as I found out from Mandy Spook one evening.

I had just finished eating dinner when Mandy tapped me on the shoulder.

'Fancy a beer, Seán?' In the otherwise empty bar, she blew off some steam.

'This thing with Colombia has become a nightmare. We've been re-tasked to gather everything we have on both

Monaghan and McCauley – all known associates, any devices planted in places where they might frequent. We've been digging through the database too and Colin isn't letting up on us either, the workload is at breaking point. So just to warn you: you're going to get a request from HQ, too, and Colin isn't going to like it.'

Just as well I took the opportunity that night to have a few extra beers, because as Mandy Spook had said, the next morning things got a little crazy. Gary Opso from HQ in Lisburn rang on the secure telephone. My head was pounding from the night before, but with Alan away on leave it was down to me to act on the request. And what a request it was!

'There's a training operation running and we want you to put together a surveillance fit-out package for six vehicles and six operators. Cannibalise what you need from the vehicles you have. You're going to be down a few operators for a while anyway, so you should be able to manage. I want a full set of body communications kit for everyone and the really good covert vehicle cameras you have. There'll be some flight cases delivered to you this evening. Can you have it all stripped out and ready within forty-eight hours?'

As I wrote the list down, all that was going through my head was, Colin is going to go ballistic and I'll be the one in the firing line.

'Are you asking me or telling me, Gary?'

He laughed. 'I guess I'm telling you, Seán, but don't think I don't appreciate it.'

'I don't suppose you need a tech for this training operation, do you? My Spanish isn't too bad.'

'No, I don't need a tech, I'm afraid, but if I do I'll let you know.' With that he hung up and I got to work figuring out where I was going to steal this kit from.

When, instead of ringing from the operations room, Colin made the journey across the compound himself, you knew he was either extremely bored or you were in the shit. I knew that morning which it was.

'What has Gary asked for, Seán?' he almost spat at me. He really was pissed off. I listed what I had been told to put together, all the while watching Colin shake his head in response to each item. When I finally finished, he simply said, 'No way.'

Now I was in a serious predicament. Colin was my operations officer and my direct boss, but Gary was the JCU-NI operations officer for the whole of Northern Ireland, and they each wanted completely different things from me.

'Let me put a package together, Colin,' I pleaded. 'I'll keep the stripping of existing vehicle fits to a minimum and I'll give them a basic covert-camera selection from what I've got on the shelves.' I was desperate to think of ways to avoid a conflict.

'All right,' came his very welcome reply. 'But I want to see the list before it's sent out,' he added. After a pause, he asked, 'Do you know what all this is about?'

I shook my head and tried to look innocent. Colin smiled.

'Bullshit. I don't think there is a single person in this Det who doesn't know what's going on.'

I spent the next two days putting together what could only be described as a hodgepodge of covert-surveillance equipment. Despite occasional visits from the chosen operators letting me know their preferences, I had kept things very basic. I was banking on their flight cases being loaded on the plane unopened so the team would only see what they had once they'd arrived at their destination. I would take the heat from Gary when the time came. Unfortunately, the time came right away as who should be the driver who pulled up outside the tech bay to collect the flight cases, only Gary himself.

'Let's have a look and see what we've got then, Seán,' he suggested. I popped the locks and he began to look through the assorted array of covert equipment. 'Is this the best you can give me? I thought North Det had a better technical selection than this. In fact, I know they do.' 'Well, seeing as it's only a training operation, I thought a mix and match of stuff would fit the bill.'

Gary stared at me until I was worried, and then he grinned. 'I bet Colin has been giving you hell. Anyhow, it will do just fine for where we are going.'

Sharon filled me in on her two-month long adventure in Colombia. The operators had begun by teaching the Colombians the basics of surveillance, how to track a vehicle without being spotted and such like. They soon realised the Colombians were in no shape to fight the coming insurgency.

'Apart from the mess of their surveillance infrastructure, their biggest problem is corruption. It goes right to the very top, even within the ranks of the intelligence service itself. FARC can throw so much money at everything and everyone that you don't know who's been bought off and who hasn't. They're completely clueless when it comes to covert urban surveillance. They approach it like it's a military operation and that just doesn't work. They did pick up on what we taught them pretty quick but they lack the equipment to back it up, and they would need years of Det help to bring everything up to speed. I'm not sure that there is the appetite or the capacity for that from JCU-NI. There's no doubt that IRA members have been training FARC, though: some of the devices that have been found and used have all the hallmarks of an IRA unit.'

Sharon was right about the influence of the IRA on FARC attacks. In the years that followed, the number of reported attacks that could only have come from IRA knowledge made that clear:

7 August, 2002: minutes before Álvaro Uribe was inaugurated as president of Colombia, two mortar shells explode in Bogotá, killing at least fifteen and injuring forty.

15 February, 2003: a bomb, planted by FARC in an attempt to kill President Uribe, blew up a house in Neiva, killing seventeen people. The exploded house was near the airport and under the flight path of the president's plane.

4 August, 2004: a car bomb killed nine policemen in Andinápolis.

1 February, 2005: gas cylinder bombs smuggled into a marine base by Colombian marine sympathisers of FARC killed fifteen soldiers and injured twenty-five.

3 February, 2005: FARC blew up a bridge in Putumayo Department, killing eight soldiers and a civilian.

19 October, 2006: a car-bomb in the car park of Bogotá's Nueva Granada military university injured eighteen people.

9 April, 2006: one person died and thirty-four others were injured when a bomb was detonated in front of the police headquarters in Cali.

9 May, 2006: nine police officers were killed by a FARC bomb in Santander province.

10 May, 2006: a bomb killed ten Colombian soldiers in Valle del Cauca province.

10 August, 2007: an explosion in the north of Colombia's capital Bogotá wounded ten people.

1 September, 2008: four people were killed and around twenty-six more were wounded by a car bomb in the Colombian city of Cali.

FARC would carry out even more attacks in the style of the IRA in the coming years, killing and wounding indiscriminately. They were bringing the same terror to Colombia as the IRA had brought to Northern Ireland.

The entire affair had been a huge embarrassment to Sinn Féin, the Irish government and British Intelligence at a time when the peace process was still so fragile. It provided more evidence that the IRA was still active in fundraising and training – something JCU-NI already knew, and that British Intelligence was still active in Northern Ireland – something we at North Det knew even better.

11 SHERIFF'S MOUNTAIN

'Very few people outside of 2 SCT know what we do,' he confided, 'and that includes most of the rest of JCU-NI, so keep it to yourself please, mate; I'd hate to end up in Colchester prison.'

*

I didn't need the tannoy announcement to tell me there was something wrong. The piercing siren that had sounded over the radio network and out through my speaker in the tech bay had told me right away and I was immediately on my feet.

I sprinted from the workshops across the compound to the already full operations room. The alarm that had set off the siren was one that did not sound on-site but only back at base via our radio network. The different tone was telling me that one of our surveillance-camera locations had been breached.

Colin and Tom, the assistant operations officer (A/Opso), were already sitting at the camera controllers in front of the CCTV monitor wall, with various spooks and operators lined up behind them to see what was happening.

'Sheriff's Mountain is gone, Seán, both cameras, and we have an alarm going off on-site,' Colin explained, as I pushed my way in to sit beside him. I wasn't too worried just yet; it was often operator error that resulted in the overt cameras not coming online, and it was possible that a crew from either the Cameras or Radios sections at Lisburn had

85

entered the site without letting North Det know. But as I went through my checks quickly, it soon became clear that there was something seriously wrong at the location. I directed another North Det camera, mounted on a mast at Rosemount in the city, towards Sheriff's Mountain. Its 2km range would allow me to see exactly what was going on. I think nearly everyone in the room said the same thing when the image appeared on the screen: 'Holy Shit!' Sheriff's Mountain was under attack … in real time, as it were.

There, right in front of us – thanks to the camera link – were approximately twenty men dressed in anoraks and balaclavas launching an attack on the mast and adjacent reinforced concrete communications hut. They had used bolt cutters to get through the lock on the gates to the site and gain access to this highly secure JCU-NI installation. They were armed with sledgehammers, too, and were now in the process of gaining entry to the communications hut, hence the alarm over the North Det radio network.

It was a few moments before anyone reacted. Colin shouted over his shoulder to Gill Lo, the TCG liaison officer: 'Get TCG on the line, and get whatever PSNI patrols they have in the area over there now!' Even as his instructions came, things were getting worse. The mob was now into the communications hut and began to toss fireworks inside, followed by tyres covered in flammable liquid set alight. Other cameras on the monitor wall began to drop out as the mob turned its attention to the mast itself. Because they couldn't get past the locked gate at the base of the mast, they was using the sledgehammers and wire cutters to hack away at the exposed cables running from the mast to the communications hut.

Moments later, the sirens of the approaching PSNI patrols caused the gang to abort the attack and make their escape across the fields towards the safety of the staunchly Republican Creggan estate. Before they left, they dowsed the cables in more flammable liquid, leaving the site ablaze with billowing thick black smoke.

The entire attack had been witnessed by a reporter and photographer from the *Derry News* newspaper who had received an anonymous phone call inviting him to attend 'a demonstration' at the site. Some demonstration! More like full-scale assault.

Sheriff's Mountain was of huge strategic importance to North Det and now it was seriously damaged. It had two high-powered overt-surveillance cameras mounted on its mast, which provided not only a view of the Creggan area of Derry city but also of the surrounding countryside. There were several North Det targets operating within the radius of those cameras and now we had no way to remotely track those targets. That problem on its own could be overcome, but the site played a much more important role as well: it was the hub for the fibre-optic network relaying images from many of the other overt cameras not only in Derry city but in Strabane, Omagh and the border areas. As a result of the sabotage, North Det had lost perhaps its most valuable and potent surveillance tools.

Three other possible results from the attack occurred to me as I sat at the controls, which together could render North Det blind and deaf in surveillance terms. First, dozens of covert cameras dotted around Derry city and the surrounding area, which beamed their images to microwave dishes mounted on the mast at Sheriff's Mountain and from there through the encrypted fibre-optic network back to North Det, could be disrupted. It was possible that both their live images and the ability to control those cameras were now gone. Second, those many listening and tracking devices placed in houses, vehicles and weapons hides transmitting back via Sheriff's Mountain could be gone. Third (and this one I didn't dare even voice), there could be the loss of all radio communications within Derry city.

The PSNI patrols were now joined by the fire engines battling the blaze at the communications hut and the base of the mast. Colin looked over his shoulder at the gathered crowd. 'What are you all doing here? Get out on the fucking ground! We still have work to do, it's just back to basics for a while. Let's see how good you really are.' The room emptied within seconds, leaving only Colin, Jamie Pronto, and me.

'How bad, Seán?' Colin said, close to a whisper.

'I honestly don't know, until I can get out there for a look, but it's not looking good from here. We've obviously lost the cameras at Sheriff's, and both Strabane and Omagh are offline too. That's just what I've checked. I'll have to go through every overt and covert camera in the matrix.' I knew Colin's main concern would be the covert cameras, and in particular the one that covered Harvey Street in the Bogside area of the city.

Meanwhile, I was so focused on reviewing the cameras and on the conversation with Colin that I wasn't paying attention to the radio network. It was only when Mark, the duty bleep, stuck his head in to say he had no communications with any of the operators on the ground beyond Ebrington Barracks, that my worst fears were realised.

'What do we need to do here?' asked Colin, directing the question at me and Jamie.

'We'll need as many teams as possible from Cameras and Radios at Lisburn on standby, but I think we need an assessment before we can do much,' I replied. Jamie nodded in agreement.

'Okay, whatever you need. I'll make a few calls now to make sure HQ knows this is priority one. Briefing in an hour and we'll go from there.' As we were leaving, Colin grabbed me by the arm and took me aside.

'What about Harvey Street, Seán? Have we lost it?'

'We have images coming back but no control of the camera. The good news is that the camera is trained in on the front door, so we can still monitor who's coming and going.'

'Once you've done the assessment, I want you down at Masonic tonight getting that camera online. Let the other techs handle the rest.' I realised Colin was making sure that no one coming in from outside to help in our hour of need would be privy to where his coverts were. 'We're short on operators, Seán. That "training exercise" has left me four operators down, and there's another on leave; I need those eyes back as soon as possible.' He wasn't one to panic but this was clearly a major problem.

I made my way back over to the tech bay to put in a call to the Camera and Radio sections at Lisburn to warn them what was coming down the line. Before I could even hit the speed-dial button on the secure telephone, it was already ringing. It wasn't anyone I might have been expecting, but Mark, an old mate of mine from 14th Signal Regiment, now assistant pronto with 2 SCT, the Couriers, in Moscow camp, Belfast: the unit that Howes and Wood had served with. I knew Mark well. It had, in fact, been me that had suggested to him that he go to JCU-NI, but I hadn't heard from him since I had arrived at the unit.

'I'm in the shit, Seán,' he said. 'The lads are due out on the ground shortly and I have no radio communications with the vehicles. The pronto is away on leave and I need to get it sorted.' I could hear the panic in his voice, but to be honest I really didn't understand why. They were simply moving documents from one point to another, weren't they? A loss of radio communications didn't matter that much in such a situation. They were, after all, armed. I tried to calm Mark down and get him off the line. I had my own, much bigger, problems to deal with.

'It's not that big a deal, mate. They probably don't use

their radios that much anyway, so don't sweat it.' I was looking at the clock on the wall, conscious that my hour until the briefing was ticking away.

'It's not quite that simple, Seán. Help me out of this one, and I'll fill you in later.' Now he had my interest, so I ran him through some fault-finding steps until we had the system back up and running.

'Cheers, mate. A few beers down at Lisburn next weekend? My shout!' Before I could answer he was gone, and I went about making my own calls.

Ted from Cameras and Henry from Radios were in the packed briefing room along with Richard, the officer-in-command who had sent me here, all having arrived by helicopter from Lisburn a few minutes earlier. Colin began.

'As you all know, there was an attack at Sheriff's Mountain today and we need to get what we've lost back online. We have since learned that the attack was launched by Real IRA members, headed by our old friend from Strabane. We don't want to draw attention to the fact that the site is of any importance to us, so the PSNI have sent out a statement to the press saying the station is used by the emergency services and the damage could have very serious consequences for delivering those services. That should muddy the waters a bit. If we pile in there with too many bodies they will know they hit a nerve.

'Seán, you and Ted will head to Sheriff's later this evening to assess the damage. You'll be dressed as PSNI officers and taken in by a TCG patrol. The operators will provide cover for you on the ground, both for the assessment and the repair phase later tonight. Right, get to it!' Colin 's briefings were always short and sharp.

Ted and I headed for a room at the back of the operations building where there were wardrobes filled with all manner of uniforms and clothes, including the very latest PSNI uniform in a full range of sizes. Once we were dressed, we made our way to the armoury and selected a Glock 17 pistol each, the one used by the PSNI. Now looking the part, we made the journey to the site.

It was bad. The entire inside of the hut was scorched and stank of burnt rubber and petrol. At first glance it looked like a lot of damage had been done, but on closer inspection they fortunately hadn't managed to damage some of the main equipment stored in secure cabinets at the rear of the hut. The damage to the cables on the mast was, however, extensive and would certainly render the cameras offline for a few days. It would be down to the maintenance crews from Cameras and Radios to replace the damaged equipment and cables as quickly as possible. Crews would have to be sent to each of the other camera sites that had been affected, to reboot their systems. That should be enough to bring everything back up and running, I concluded. We arrived back at the Det in time to meet the maintenance crews, their vehicles packed with spares, and brief them on what had to be done that night.

Next, I got my own rigging kit ready for the trip to Masonic, with Fred Op accompanying me as additional security. Masonic was located close to the courthouse in Derry city, a small army post with a mast that overlooked the Bogside Inn and the surrounding streets. North Det had three cameras mounted on the mast, two overt and one covert, the covert being the most important of the three.

I was slightly apprehensive as I drove the tech vehicle through the city that Saturday at about 0100: never a good time to be approaching an army base and certainly not one located right in the heart of Derry. There were still a lot of people milling about the streets but, as usual, the soldiers inside Masonic were on the ball, so as I swung the vehicle in towards the gates, they opened immediately and two soldiers ran out to provide cover as we entered.

Rigging itself was hazardous, too. Not only was it difficult to see in the dark using just a torch with an infrared filter, also at the back of your mind was the threat that you could be seen by someone who might want to take a pot shot from the ground with a firework or petrol bomb. I didn't waste any time, quickly scaling the mast and balancing myself out on one of the beams to work on the covert camera. The position of the mast gave an excellent view of the Bogside but it also gave the Bogside an excellent view of me and, camera rebooted, I got my ass down with a sense of relief.

By 0500 everyone was back at North Det and most of the cameras and communications were repaired. Within a few days everything was back to normal. As far as we know, Real IRA never knew how close they had come to disabling British Intelligence in the Derry area. Had they persisted with their attack and destroyed the communications hut completely, they would have been able to operate unobserved for weeks. The editor of the *Derry News*, Garbhan Downey, was later summoned to court and ordered to hand over all photo negatives, prints, digital images and the computer disc relating to the attack.

There was one loose end in the episode. I still had to get the story behind Mark's unusual behaviour, and so the following Saturday night I arranged to meet him at Thiepval Barracks in Lisburn for the few drinks he had promised. The Green Fly bar was run by the intelligence corps and was one of the favourite haunts of JCU-NI personnel. Mark was already there when I arrived, a girl called Katie from 2 SCT accompanying him. Drinks in hand, we chatted for a bit about each other's postings and where mutual friends were now until after a few more drinks I cut to the chase about the previous week.

'So, Mark, what was all the panic about?' The two greatest scourges in the British army are alcohol and secrets. The first loosens the tongue and as for the second, as soon as someone is told not to tell anyone, they need to tell someone. Such was the case here.

'2 SCT isn't what you think, Seán. Sure, they transport top-secret documents around from Det to Det but that's not their real job. All those listening devices that are planted by the Det operators, well guess who listens to them?'

It was then that Katie chipped in.

'Yeah, I spend my time stuffed in a van, in a hide in a field or if I'm lucky in a room somewhere listening to devices 24/7. The things I have to hear, guys having sex, masturbating, taking a dump or worse. Some of these guys are real perverts and should be locked up for that alone.' She caught herself and didn't elaborate any further. It was Mark who continued. 'Ninety-nine per cent of the time, there is nothing in it but now and again these guys give something away and that's what we hope for.' The rest of the night was like any other night but the following morning, before we both headed back to our respective Dets, Mark warned me not to tell anyone what they'd told me.

JCU-NI was full of secrets within secrets, many more of which I would learn the longer I spent there.

12 HELI DOWN

I brought the car down the beach and we put Fred on a spinal board and positioned him carefully on the back seat. It was only then that the three of us looked towards the dark waters of the Foyle. There, semi-submerged and upside down, was the Gazelle helicopter.

*

One thing I learned about North Det early on was that the boundaries around discipline and rules got tested quite a lot. It seemed to be just part of North Det's culture, as they say, part of what made it a unique place to work. Traditions such as the stealing of the Det Christmas tree from one of the forest parks around the area, or the use of industrial-sized foam fire extinguishers at parties, were harmless enough. You could understand where they were coming from when they tampered with each other's vehicles while they were on leave, for instance, putting talc into the car air vents or lowering the suspension so that the 'perks plates' would fire when they went over a speed bump. You might even put up with the planting of cameras and listening devices in each other's rooms, and playing them back on the monitor wall in the operations room for all to see. However, sometimes North Det pushed things too far and there were serious consequences both for individuals and for the Det as a whole.

The leaving party for our colleague Gerry Op, one of our 'shakey' troopers, was in full swing at 0300 hours on a Friday

in mid-July as Alan and I arrived back from Altnagelvin
Hospital, having just installed a covert camera there. Alan
asked if I was okay with him heading to the bar for a few
drinks. Happy to take the duty pager for this one, I headed
to the operations room to hand in our weapons and let the
bleep on duty know that I was on call for the rest of the
night. As I passed the bar I could hear bottles smashing and
the sounds of lads playing '9mm darts'. (This involved using
pistols instead of darts and aiming at a replica dartboard
painted on one of the walls in the bar.) North Det's parties
were always extreme affairs but that night it seemed they
were out to set new records.

The operations room was quiet as I checked the board to
see which operators were on emergency response duty, the
'crash-out team' as we called it. With Colin on leave, Tom
A/Opso was meant to be in charge but he was in the bar with
the rest – something Colin wouldn't have approved of. I
escaped to my quarters.

I had only just got into bed when the familiar sound of
the Gazelle helicopter engine whining into life drifted across
the compound to my room. That's odd, I thought, there was
no standby order over the tannoy, so there couldn't have
been an emergency. Nor had there been any routine flights
planned for that night. I leaped up in time to see the
helicopter rise above the security fencing and head across
the airfield. I must have drifted off to sleep, I reasoned, and
somehow missed the call. I dressed quickly and made my
way to the operations building.

I was met by George, the longest-serving operator at
North Det, who had also been woken by the Gazelle taking
off.

'Crash-out, George?' I asked. He shook his head.

'Not that I know of, mate, I'll check with the duty bleep
now.' The duty bleep knew about as much as we did: in other
words, nothing. George asked him to get the helicopter on

the radio net and we went to check the board to see who was the duty pilot that evening. Tonight the pilot was – George and I exchanged a knowing look – Phil. Shit! We both knew that could well mean trouble. Rumour had it that Phil had once served with the SAS but had been kicked out due to some incident in Russia, of which no one knew the details. He was, apparently, forced to retrain to become a pilot with the Army Air Corps and ended up at JCU-NI. Whatever the truth, he had a reputation as a wild one and some of the Opsos wouldn't have him at their Dets at all. Colin seemed okay with him, though, able to manage his wilder side. Problem was: Colin was away, and something wasn't right.

After fifteen minutes of fruitless efforts to raise the Gazelle over the radio net, George decided to get serious.

'Seán, you get over to the bar and find someone who knows where he's gone. I'll stay here and keep trying to get him on the radio.' I hated going into the bar when I was sober and everyone else had been drinking all night but I knew it had to be done. I managed to corner Alan at one end of the bar; the rest of the group was a lost cause.

'Any idea where Phil has gone with the heli, Alan?' Alan had a big stupid grin on his face.

'Yeah,' he sniggered, 'him and Fred are gone for a spin. Crazy!'

Shit, I thought. I grabbed the 'honesty book' and looked down the list until I found their names. Phil and Fred had signed to pay for five bottles of red wine between them that night. This was seriously serious.

It was normal for the pilots to have a few drinks when the working day was done at the Dets. Despite the rules around alcohol and flying, most Opsos turned a blind eye to such things. It's not like anyone was going to come into the Det and breathalyse operators. But it often went beyond a few drinks at North Det. Being the most insular Det in JCU-NI, there was almost an atmosphere of invincibility among some, and it was often their downfall.

'Why didn't you stop them, you fucking idiot?' I screamed at Alan. He just gave me a gormless shrug. By now the rest of the bar had quietened down, the music was switched off and I noticed George standing at the door.

'Everyone: out! Anyone on the crash-out team to the operations room! Everyone else to your beds. Now! Seán, can you bring all the cameras up on the monitor wall? Let's see if we can spot them in the air.'

Back in the operations room, with me getting all our cameras online to scan the skyline for the telltale flashing strobe light, the assistant operations officer, Tom was causing problems. Even though he was so drunk he could barely see, never mind control the cameras, he was insisting on taking over. Next, Simon OC arrived, woken from his sleep by the duty bleep. He wanted to contact HQ in Lisburn right away and start a full-scale search, but George, once an experienced operations officer himself (though now more of an adviser than an operator), held fast.

'No need for that yet. Let's see how the situation develops first and try to keep it in house. Tom, get to your bed and sleep it off, you're no good to me in your condition.' Neither man questioned him, the glare in George's eyes told them that he wouldn't brook any arguments at this moment. 'Seán, get back on the cameras and find those guys.' I scanned the skies around Derry, Strabane and Omagh for the next two hours, but spotted nothing.

By 0600, we were coming around to the belief that the situation was lost and that we would have to raise the alarm, when the intercom at the rear entrance to the compound buzzed. I had never in all my time at North Det heard it sound before and I immediately switched to the camera covering the gate. There on the screen was Phil, huddled over in a very dishevelled state. Two of the operators took off at speed for the gate and carried him to the sick bay at the far end of the building. Besides some broken ribs and bad bruises he wasn't in too bad shape, and with great difficulty he gave us a rough indication of where Fred was.

Within minutes, two operator vehicles raced from the compound, Big Rick and I in one and Lee in the other. Lee was already on the radio net to the duty bleep, telling him to get the main gates of the camp open because he had no intention of stopping when he got there. We sped through and turned towards Derry-city, taking a side road a few miles along that led to the beaches of the Foyle estuary. Though we were travelling at incredible speed, I had every confidence in both men's abilities behind the wheel. At the shoreline, we split in opposite directions. Suddenly, about 200 metres in front of us, we spotted a bundle on the beach. We took off on foot, sprinting, and as we got closer it was obvious that the bundle was Fred. He wasn't moving. I started switching the torch I was carrying on and off in the direction that Lee had taken, while Big Rick set to work on Fred. He looked lifeless, and I had a sinking feeling in my stomach that we may have been too late. When Lee arrived, both operators got Fred stabilised quickly. They immediately identified a broken leg, but more worryingly also felt there was some spinal damage. I brought the car down the beach and we put Fred Op on a spinal board (which all the operators carried in the boot of their vehicles as part of their first aid kits) and positioned him carefully on the back seat. It was only then that the three of us looked towards the dark waters of the Foyle. There, semi-submerged and upside down, was the Gazelle helicopter.

With Fred stabilised and in the back of the car, we headed straight for Altnagelvin Hospital at a very slow speed to avoid sudden jolts. We pulled up outside A&E and the staff, forewarned by the Det's TCG contacts, were waiting to admit Fred. It was time for Big Rick and Lee to disappear, to avoid being compromised. I remained with Fred until someone from HQ arrived, staying close by, part-security – still armed – for a comrade but more so as a very concerned friend. It was the first time in my army career that I had come close to losing a mate and it wasn't a good feeling.

Within the hour I was replaced by two plain-clothes soldiers from The Prince of Wales Own Regiment of Yorkshire, both armed with pistols discreetly hidden under their jackets. They would remain to guard Fred for the remainder of his stay at the hospital. I was picked up by one of the operators and taken back to the Det. Now to hear from Phil on how exactly the Gazelle ended up in the Foyle.

Apparently, Fred had mentioned trying for the army air corps pilots' course, and it was this simple statement that started the whole disastrous episode. Phil offered to take Fred up for a lesson and both agreed there was no time like the present. Despite the intoxication, the flight had gone okay and they were almost back at Ballykelly when, amazingly, Phil decided it would be a good idea to hand the stick over to Fred and let him get a feel for what it's like to control an aircraft. Drunk, flying in the dark and completely unfamiliar with the controls, Fred became disorientated and the helicopter plunged. Phil's reactions were too slowed by the alcohol for him to react in time to pull the aircraft up from the dive. As it hit the water it overturned, trapping the men in their seats below the waterline. The icy-cold water of the Foyle flooded in.

Irrespective of training for such a scenario, it's quite a different matter when something like that actually happens, and happens at a time when your mind is dulled by alcohol. Nonetheless, Phil managed to free himself and reach the surface. He scanned the water for Fred Op but saw no sign. At great risk to himself, and despite his own injuries, he went back down below the water and managed to free the unconscious Fred from his seat before dragging him to the beach. He then made his way along the shoreline to

Shackleton Barracks at Ballykelly. No matter how stupid he was to go up in the chopper in the first place, I had to admire his response to the disaster.

It was time for North Det to close ranks and cover up. The team geared up for what it thought would be an internal investigation by JCU-NI HQ in Lisburn. In fact, it turned out to be far worse than that. For the first time in its history – thanks to Phil and Fred – North Det had to stomach an external investigation, one headed by the army air corps air-crash investigations unit and supported by the Royal Military Police (RMP). Thankfully, we did not have to face this investigation alone. At JCU-NI HQ was someone we called the 'flying lawyer', a lawyer who provided legal advice and representation in the case of incidents involving Det operators. It was usually for shootings in difficult circumstances, though, not self-inflicted helicopter crashes!

We began by destroying evidence: the honesty book from the bar was shredded and then incinerated for good measure, the bar was cleaned until it was sparkling, and all recorded evidence of what actually happened was done away with. Meanwhile, George and Simon OC stalled for time to make sure that everyone could get their stories straight. They told the investigation team that operational tasks would, unfortunately, prevent any of North Det's personnel being available for interview for a few days, and that Fred and Phil were in no fit state to be interviewed yet. At the same time, the 'flying lawyer' was tying the investigators up in technical legal matters.

The air-crash investigators and the RMP were pushing to get access to North Det's compound, but that could simply never be allowed to happen. And so the decision was made that any interviews would be held in the main buildings of Shackleton Barracks. By the time it came to my interview with the RMP personnel, a couple of the other guys had already been through and I knew what to expect.

I had also been briefed on what I could and couldn't say, so just like it was for the others, this was going to be a very short interview. I sat across from the female RMP sergeant, a stern-looking woman.

'On the night of the crash, were you in the bar?'

I cleared my throat. 'No.'

She started to write. 'Where were you, then?'

'I'm afraid I can't answer that,' I answered. She looked up in disgust, clearly having had the same response from the others.

'Okay, did you hear the helicopter taking off?'

'I'm afraid I can't answer that.' This went on for about twenty minutes, until finally the 'flying lawyer' made it clear that I had nothing further to add to the investigation. And so it went for the other thirty or so members of the Det who were interviewed, much to the frustration of the investigators, you can be sure.

Eventually, the investigation fizzled out and at a hearing in April 2005 it was found that the pilot was 'probably under the influence of alcohol'. And while the army said that Phil had been court-martialled and banned from flying, he was in fact still flying, just not at JCU-NI. The official report said he was 'disorientated due to a lack of attention to flight instruments'. There was no mention of Fred being at the controls when the aircraft went down. The report also said that Phil was distracted and fatigued due to extensive operational duties. Phil had admitted to drinking between one and two glasses of wine at a social event five hours before the accident. He also admitted to taking off without the appropriate authorisation from the detachment commander and without being briefed. The report pointed out that neither men had been wearing flight suits, a fact that had never been properly explained.

Unfortunately, though he was very lucky to survive, Fred (referred to at the hearing as the co-pilot) suffered serious back injuries and a broken leg. He was eventually discharged from the British army on medical grounds. I went to visit him at his home in Wales a few months after. His life was in tatters. He could barely move, was in constant pain, and had separated from his wife.

'A moment of madness, Seán, and it ruined everything. I've lost it all. Now I'm just a useless drunk, waiting to see out my days.'

To my shame, I never went back to see Fred Op again. I wanted to remember the man that I had known, full of life and a sense of fun, not the broken man he had become.

13 YOU'RE NICKED

'This is bullshit. This guy's definitely a no-show. Can I get out of here now?' Will, one of the operators, was moaning again from the boot of the 'amnesia' vehicle.

An amnesia vehicle was so called because it was driven to a location by one of the operators, parked, and left there to give the appearance of being just another vehicle and forgotten about. However, this being espionage, inside the boot was another operator engaged in surveillance on a target. It was a great tactic in terms of results – it seemed people took little notice of visibly empty vehicles. It was not so great in terms of comfort.

To be fair to Will, he has been in there for almost ten hours at this stage, operating the covert video camera which was trained on the target house through the opaque vehicle number plate, and using the concealed, remotely operated stills cameras dotted around the vehicle to snap anyone coming and going. Unfortunately, Will's urine bags, now probably full and leaking a little all the time, combined with the heat of that particular day to make the boot a fairly unpleasant place to be.

I laughed to myself back in the tech bay as I listened on the network to the other operator's jokes made at Will's expense.

*

Our Charlie One was John Paul Hannan, a member of a Louth- and Fermanagh-based Real IRA active service unit responsible for a bombing campaign in England during

2001: at BBC offices in Wood Lane, White City, on 3 March; in Ealing, west London, on 3 August; and in Birmingham on 3 November. The four other members of the bombing unit, James McCormack, Noel Maguire and Aiden and Robert Hulme, had already appeared at the Old Bailey in connection with the attacks. Other gang members were caught after police raids on a Yorkshire farmhouse, the result of a tip-off from an elderly woman who became suspicious of the strangers after seeing e-fits of them on television Hannan was the only member left at large, and the task to find him fell to us.

From information gleaned from informers, it was known that Hannan was mostly moving from safe house to safe house in the Republic, but on occasion was taken across the border to visit relatives in Newtownbutler, Co. Fermanagh. This was a good start, but unfortunately the informer couldn't give his handler a precise day or time that Hannan would cross into Northern Ireland. Of course, North Det couldn't mount a prolonged operation in Newtownbutler. It was just too small a place and strangers would stand out. Instead, we deployed a 'green army unit', our dedicated Prince of Wales Own Regiment of Yorkshire's close observation platoon (COP), to monitor the area for us. When the COP reported seeing a number of men visiting the target house and thought it was possible that Charlie One was on his way, it was time for North Det to take over again.

On the morning of Friday, 5 July 2002, a briefing was called prior to the arrival of the TCG personnel. This was the usual procedure: North Det would put its plan together in isolation, then brief TCG on what they needed to know and do later.

'Hannan has been on the run in the Republic since last year. There is a chance, if only a slight one, that he may visit relatives in Newtownbutler this weekend. Given the size of the place, you don't have to be told how difficult it's going to be to operate, so this won't be a long, drawn-out operation. If it looks like going on more than a few days, we'll pull out and hand it back to COP. It's as close to the border as we get, and we may have to stray over into the Republic to keep any surveillance that we pick up going. Anyone got any problems with that?'

He was asking the operators but I think he was sounding me out, too. I wasn't sure how I felt about it, really. It wouldn't be an accidental incursion, which often happened, but a pre-planned infringement of heavily armed undercover soldiers into the Republic. I kept quiet just the same and let the briefing go on.

'You all know we are down a number of operators due to a "training operation". Even Colin couldn't keep a straight face as the room filled with muffled coughs of 'Bullshit!'

'Anyhow, it won't make things any easier. With the chance of being compromised so high, I'm going to keep the number of operator vehicles within the area to a minimum until the last minute, when we are ready to close in. I'll be using cameras and specialist kit where possible. Right Techs, what have we got available?'

I waited for Alan to speak, but as was becoming usual, he stayed quiet, so I started to rattle off what we had that would be appropriate and could be used to fill the gap.

'We have two plumbers' vans fitted with four surveillance cameras. There are a good few building jobs going on down there at the moment, so they should blend in. The two motorbikes are fitted with covert cameras so we have that option, and the drivers' faces won't be seen. I've just had a new thermal-imaging camera sent to us on trial, might be worth giving that a shot. We have two overt cameras in the area which will give you a good overview of the approaches.'

The decision was made to set up temporary operations in Saint Angelo Barracks, Enniskillen, which was close enough to be able to get to the target quickly but far enough away that locals wouldn't see the operators coming and going. Alan went with them on this occasion. Earlier in my time there, I would have wanted to be the one deployed with the operators, but more settled now and due out on leave that weekend anyhow, it suited me just fine. Besides, it was much easier to be at the Det running things with Colin than down in bandit country with the action, where the radio signals would be iffy and the operators would have technical problems all the time.

On Friday afternoon, the operators arrived at Enniskillen, and got the specialist surveillance vehicles into place. I was in the operations room with Colin while the spooks were manning the intelligence database behind us in case Colin wanted information on anyone spotted by the operators. Jamie Pronto and the bleep on duty monitored the radio networks. Gill Lo had gone across the camp to act as our liaison with TCG. Everything was set.

The first vehicle inserted was one of the plumber's van. Colin pointed on the map to where he wanted it positioned and looked to me for a nod on whether we could receive a signal back from there. The operator, Jack, was driving it as he looked most like a plumber. Colin took control of one of the high cameras and zoomed in to where Jack was parking up, ensuring the vehicle was where he wanted it. Two of the other operators, Kevin and Damien, were providing a security cordon and would pick Jack up once he was finished. There were four cameras within the van covering practically every angle of the street. As Jack powered each one up, I confirmed to Colin that we had images and control of each camera. Before he left the van, Jack armed the Hardtac alarm system and engaged the concealed engine cut-off switch, which prevented the vehicle from starting should an attempt be made to steal it.

Next were the 'amnesia' vehicles. Each of the operators would take a stint in the boot until the operation was complete, and they would switch between the two amnesia vehicles available. First to go in was Baz Op. He got into the boot of the car at Saint Angelo Barracks in Enniskillen and made the first of his communications checks. Due to the space constraints, he wasn't carrying his usual complement of weapons, just a 9mm pistol and a couple of spare magazines. He would rely on the other operators getting to him swiftly should anything go wrong.

Once in the boot he was in for a rough ride until the vehicle was parked up in its final location. It was always the same during an 'amnesia' insertion, and everyone was resigned to it. Whoever the driver was would invariably try to hit every bump and pothole along the way to give the poor sod in the boot a proper bouncing.

The final piece of the surveillance jigsaw, and the one I was keenest to test out, was the thermal-imaging camera. I felt that given the rural location of the target house and its proximity to the border, it was highly likely that the approach to the house would be made on foot and at night, so this would be perfect. While it would give off the heat signature of anyone approaching the house, it wasn't like in the movies in that it could not penetrate walls and windows. I had fitted it into a small Mini Metro, a complete banger, with the camera firing out through the rear vehicle number plate.

Over the next forty-eight hours, the specialist surveillance vehicles were swapped around and moved to new positions in an effort to help them blend into the background. This was augmented with occasional drive-by runs by the operators in their own vehicles or on board the surveillance motorbikes.

Not everything goes to plan in an operation, and occasionally it is the simplest of things that can compromise either an individual operator or the entire operation. Doubly so in Northern Ireland, in my experience, since the general population are so observant. Perhaps decades of conflict have made them that way. Down in the border regions they missed nothing, and so only the very best and most disciplined operators could work there for any length of time.

In this case, it was two teenage schoolgirls who were responsible for taking Big Rick out. He was coming to the last six months of his tour at the Det and was now a vastly experienced covert-surveillance operator. He really didn't look like a soldier at all, heavily bearded and with long hair, so he definitely wouldn't have been identified under normal circumstances. However, on this occasion he forgot (as the others did from time to time) about his accent, which screamed 'Brit' and therefore 'soldier' to most people in Northern Ireland.

He stopped at a garage on the outskirts of Newtownbutler to get fuel and – against Det regulations – took a call on his personal phone just as two young girls were entering the shop. As he was going in to pay, he heard one of the girls say to the owner, 'Careful, that's a Brit soldier out there' and, just like that, Big Rick was compromised.

With Big Rick now back at the Det, Colin was running out of options. We had already been deployed in the town for two days and it being now a Monday morning, people were starting to go about their normal business again. His operators would start to stick out.

'A couple more hours and we'll call it a day,' he announced over the radio net.

'Thank God for that!' Will Op, a sergeant in the Royal Marines and also on his first tour at JCU-NI, whispered down the net.

Having heard the announcement of the extraction, I made my way over to the operations room to see if anything was needed from me before I headed off on leave. The operators were getting ready to pull out, when in a barely audible whisper we heard 'Standby! Standby!' It was Will. 'Eyes on Charlie One approaching target.'

Hannan had not arrived on foot, as expected, but by car. This caused an avalanche of activity. Colin began to redirect the operators to the target house while bringing all the cameras up on the monitor wall again. He told Gill over at TCG to get their officers ready to move in when ordered.

Unfortunately, Hannan was already in the house by the time everything was in place – we had lost the opportunity of taking him outside, which is always a much cleaner and safer option. It would have to be a forced entry for the arrest on this occasion, even with the possibility of someone inside the house being armed. Colin decided that the operators would carry out the forced entry before handing over to TCG and withdrawing.

'Go! Go! Go!' was heard and next thing vehicles screeched to a halt outside the house. Operators raced to the front door and to the back door. Using battering rams, they smashed the doors in and entered simultaneously. Systematically clearing rooms, shouting 'Police! Police! Get down!' as they did so, they made their way through the house.

Sitting at the kitchen table with some relatives was Charlie One. His face was a picture of surprise and terror. He was dragged to the floor, had his hands zip-tied behind his back and was searched.

It was all over in thirty seconds, without a shot being fired, a textbook operation from start to finish. TCG moved in and the Det operators withdrew immediately, to collect the specialist vehicles before regrouping in Enniskillen and heading back to Ballykelly.

Hannan was taken to London later that day and soon after appeared before Bow Street Magistrates Court in London for charging. At their trial in April 2003, the five men were found guilty of Terrorist Offences relating to the

London and Birmingham attacks in 2001. Robert Hulme, 23, and his brother Aiden, 25, were each jailed for twenty years. Noel Maguire, 34, who, according to the trial judge, played 'a major part in the bombing conspiracy', was sentenced to twenty-two years. All three had continuously denied conspiring to cause explosions between 1 January and 15 November 2001, as part of a Real IRA bombing campaign. James McCormack, 34, of Co. Louth, had already admitted to the charge at an earlier hearing and was found to have played the most serious part in the terror campaign. He was sentenced to twenty-two years in prison. Hannan, North Det's Charlie One, was said to have been influenced heavily by the others in the group and, given his early guilty plea and his age at the time of the bombings, was given the more lenient sentence of sixteen years in prison.

There was a huge celebration at North Det that night but I was not part of it. I was driving my own vehicle from Ballykelly, across the border at Aughnacloy, to visit my family in Cork. This was a serious breach of British army security policy, as I was supposed to first take a flight to the UK and then take another flight to Dublin or Cork. Colin was a very practical man, however, and he knew by this stage that I was well able to look after myself, so he allowed me drive home.

As I crossed the border, it was strange hearing the delayed news that John Paul Hannan had been arrested. And by the PSNI. I smiled to myself, knowing who had actually come knocking at his door that day.

14 EARLY DAYS AT NORTH DET

By this stage I had been privy to much of the intelligence surrounding the various paramilitary organisations operating in Northern Ireland. I was no longer under any illusions about them. It was clear they cared neither about the innocent lives they might destroy nor actually about the 'cause' they claimed so loudly as their justification. It was power struggle, criminality and greed above all else. But life at North Det sometimes threw things at me that I still wasn't able to process fully or that didn't sit comfortably with me about the situation.

*

There were three people who could be found each evening in the bar at North Det almost without fail: George Op, Mandy Spook and me. It was never a heavy session, just a few beers or, in George's case, a glass of red wine or two, to wind down after the day's work. George, a veteran of special duties in Northern Ireland for almost thirty years, was always good for a yarn about the good old bad days in Northern Ireland, and both Mandy and I were always keen to listen. He was in his mid-fifties by this time, and while he was one of the nicest guys you could meet, always there to point you in the right direction, he was someone I couldn't quite read fully and in whose company I never fully relaxed.

I was glad it was Mandy, then, one night in the bar on our downtime, who took the opportunity to ask a question that had been on my mind since I arrived at North. Given my background and not wanting to raise suspicions, I never liked to ask too many questions about North Det's history, but I was insatiably curious about it.

'So what was it like in the beginning, George, when the SAS and the Dets first started operating in Northern Ireland?'

He paused for a minute to take a sip of wine:

'I was first deployed to Northern Ireland in 1976, straight from the deserts of Oman where the SAS had been fighting the insurgency. I was just a young trooper then. We really didn't have much of a clue of the type of war that we would be fighting here. So, in the beginning we were treating it just like the campaign we had fought in Oman. We often got frustrated and would pull up in the street in open view, trying to lure the IRA into a firefight. We knew we could win in an open fight but they weren't that stupid; they remained in the shadows and dictated the type of campaign that would be fought. They were prepared to fight a prolonged guerrilla war, one that we weren't yet trained for. It took us a while to adapt and many mistakes were made before we got it right.'

He glanced around the bar looking for something, then pointed to a picture on the wall. It was a newspaper clipping of a wounded man lying on the ground surrounded by security forces. 'See that? That's Francis Hughes and I was part of the operation that finally captured him. It was my first big success.' I quickly grabbed another round of drinks, making sure that George would be going nowhere for a while. This one I wanted to hear!

I already knew a fair bit about the man, of course. Born in the mid-1950s into a staunchly Republican family in the Derry townland of Tamlaghtduff, or Scribe Road as it is otherwise known, he initially became involved with the Official IRA, which were strong in the South Derry area in those days, but with the signing of the unilateral ceasefire in 1972, he left the movement and set up his own independent command in the Bellaghy area. By 1973 that force, along with Hughes, had formally joined the Provisional IRA. Some years later, on 18 April 1977, Hughes, along with two other IRA volunteers, were travelling in a car near the town of Moneymore when they were intercepted by an RUC patrol. The three attempted to escape but lost control of their vehicle. They abandoned the car and opened fire on the RUC patrol, killing two officers and wounding another. The men made their escape across the fields and despite a huge search operation were able to escape. Hughes became one of the most wanted men in Northern Ireland following the incident.

In August of that year, his two accomplices were arrested but Hughes remained at large until the following year. After a gun battle in March 1978 with the SAS, Hughes was finally captured and sentenced to eighty-three years in prison. He was the second prisoner to join the 1981 hunger strikes at the Maze prison. He began his two weeks after Bobby Sands, and died after fifty-nine days without food.

It was with the details of his capture and the Special Forces' involvement that George now had me riveted.

'Hughes was giving the normal British army units and the RUC the runaround, making them look like fools. Despite the manpower they was throwing at it, they were coming up with nothing. By then there was a huge number of British troops in Northern Ireland, but it was the combination of the Dets and the SAS teams that was having the most effect on the paramilitary activities. The MRF [Military Reaction Force] or FRU or whatever you want to call it, although officially disbanded by 1978, was working well in the urban areas but rural surveillance was still very difficult for us. We didn't have all the gadgets that are available now, our surveillance cars had a basic communications fit-out if we were lucky, and there were no tracking or listening devices worth talking about. So it took men on the ground to get things done.

'We knew from a tip-off that Hughes was operating in the Maghera area and in March 1978 both the SAS units and the Det teams had covert-surveillance operations there. We were manning observation posts in fields, ditches and farm buildings while the Dets were handling covert surveillance in the nearby townlands and villages. I was part of a four-man SAS team split into two, one located in an observation post opposite a farm on the south side of the Ranaghan Road, near Maghera, the other, where I was, about a mile away.

'After a few nights of nothing, at about 2100 hours on this particular night, a sudden 'Standby! Standby!' came over the radio net from the other two. Through their night-vision scopes they had made out two armed men making their way along the trees. Both appeared to be dressed in military fatigues so, in case they were part of a normal British army or UDR (Ulster Defence Regiment) patrol, our lads opted to challenge them rather than fire. It was actually Hughes and another IRA fella. They opened fired and killed Lance Corporal David "Taff" Jones, originally of the Parachute Regiment, and injured "Benny" though not before he managed to let off a few rounds at them. It was that burst that injured Hughes in the leg, slowed him down and led to his subsequent capture.

'Meanwhile, we were listening to all this unfold on the radio net as we sprinted the mile to get to them and provide supporting fire. By the time we arrived on the scene, Hughes and his accomplice were gone. It didn't take long for the place to be flooded with troops and we began a massive search for the two men. It was a bitterly cold night, I remember, and the search continued well into the following morning. Eventually Hughes was found at about midday, though the other man slipped through our net. If it had been me or any of the other Regiment lads who found Hughes, he would have been dead there and then. Sorry, Seán, but that's how it was back then. None of us fought for queen and country or any of that shite, but we did fight for our mates and Hughes had just killed one of mine.' I could see the pain on George's face from the memory of the loss of his friend, and reckoned, given the same set of circumstances – and knowing how close I was to a lot of my colleagues – that I probably would have wanted to kill Hughes as well.

George seemed to be at ease and talkative, so I plucked up the courage to ask him about something that had been killing me to know since I first saw the clipping on the wall when I arrived.

'Will you tell us what really happened at Loughgall, George?'

'Well, you have to bear in mind, the SAS had been used to fighting mostly in open battle. Now, in the North, we were fighting a different type of enemy but some still hadn't made that change in their mindset, so sometimes when there was a clash with an IRA unit, things would get out of hand and people ended up dead unnecessarily. Things were even wilder back then. The Dets and SAS units were a law unto themselves, really. We were totally outside of the British army chain of command and were as such accountable to no one. If you think we're a clandestine operation now, back then we were blacker than black. At least we have a name these days.

'The PIRA East Tyrone Brigade was led by Paddy Kelly and they were one of the most effective and daring units the IRA ever had. They were meticulous in their planning and were such a tight-knit unit that the chance of us getting an informer in amongst them was close to zero.

'What we did have by then, though, was a huge advancement in both surveillance skills and equipment. Covert cameras and listening devices were being developed specifically for use by us in Northern Ireland and the infrastructure for the overt cameras that we now take for granted was starting to come online. We as operators were better trained, too, particularly in rural surveillance techniques and while we were still getting information from informers, we weren't so reliant on it anymore. I was also quite an experienced surveillance operator by then, but Loughgall was one of the most spectacular operations any of us would ever take part in.

'In December of '85 the East Tyrone Brigade was responsible for a major attack on the RUC barracks in Ballygawley and then in August the following year they pulled off another attack on an RUC station at The Birches. In both cases, they used the same tactics: the bases came under heavy gunfire and were then flattened by a bomb. They used a digger to transport the bomb and breach the perimeter fence, then detonated the bomb before making their escape.

'They needed to be halted. Some areas of East Tyrone and South Armagh had become virtual no-go areas for the security services because of them. Most of the men in the Brigade were already known to North Det, so it was just a case of putting them under more intense surveillance. The entire unit became Charlie One. Anything that could be bugged or tracked was targeted. Paddy Kelly and Jim Lynagh were put under the most intense surveillance I'd ever seen and monitored 24/7. But it wasn't at that level that we found our "in".

'The IRA had a huge support network at that time: vehicles were stolen for their operations by one lot, the bombs and weapons were prepared by another, and while that meant there was a distance between those who carried out the attacks and those who supplied them, it also meant that there were some who were less well trained and disciplined. And it was a slip-up by one of them that gave our surveillance teams what we needed.

'One of the operators followed a relatively low-ranking

member of the IRA unit's support team, more on a hunch than anything else, after a meeting he had with Paddy Kelly. He saw him drive past a number of locations and became suspicious when he noticed there happened to be a digger at each of them. We concluded that another attack was imminent. One of the locations was a farm near Loughgall, which was a small, mainly Protestant village. Given what an easy target the RUC station there would make, we decided that was it, and mounted an immediate surveillance operation and planned an ambush. We called in the SAS interceptor unit just because we were unsure of how many there would be in the IRA team. We knew from the previous attacks that they would be well armed and weren't afraid to use their weapons.

'Obviously, we evacuated the RUC officers from the station but we needed a decoy so a selection of SAS troops and Det operators were inserted into the station. The decision was made not to alert any of the locals in case it would scare off the IRA unit. I was part of the team of surveillance operators dotted around various observation posts in the area looking out for the IRA.

'It was still a long shot and was not looking good for us at first. We were there for days with no sign of anyone coming and in all honesty we were just about ready to call it off. Then on 6 May at about 1900, a blue van was driven into the village. After passing the RUC station a number of times, it disappeared only to arrive back a few minutes later with the digger following. We were all systems go.

'As per our plan, we let the digger break through the fencing, then as the IRA unit piled out of the van we engaged. Once we could see that the men had weapons, it was open season and everyone took the opportunity. We were armed to the teeth with everything from assault rifles to general-purpose machine guns, and soon there were hundreds of rounds raining down on the targets.

'Things did get out of hand, no doubt about it. The official reports afterwards said there were 600 rounds fired, but in reality I'd say it was probably at least twice that. Some of the lads were double-tapping more for show than anything else.

'We were so engrossed in hitting the eight men, though, that we forgot about the digger bomb. That went off suddenly with a deafening noise and the explosion pretty much destroyed the station. Some of the lads inside were injured but nothing too bad. Once we knew they were okay, we were actually all pissing ourselves laughing that the station had been blown up after all.'

'So there was no mole involved at all?' I asked.

'It was just good surveillance and nothing else, whatever the rumours might say about it.' George was adamant. 'Of course, that didn't stop the IRA's own internal security squad looking for a rat, ruthless bastards that they were.

'There was talk of an inquiry on us, too, which we were keen to avoid, of course. It would have looked very bad. We probably could have taken them prisoner but, on the other hand, we felt a long overdue message had been sent to the IRA.'

At first, the Det had seen it as the taking out of eight enemy terrorists and one of the IRA's most effective units. However, it soon became clear that in killing Declan Arthurs (21), Seamus Donnelly (19), Tony Gormley (25), Eugene Kelly (25), Patrick Kelly (30), Jim Lynagh (31), Padraig McKearney (32) and Gerard O'Callaghan (29), they had created martyrs for the cause.

All the focus about Loughgall among my community at home had been on the deaths of these eight IRA men; even the civilian, Anthony Hughes (36), didn't get much of a mention. The fact that they were attempting to drive a bomb into a manned police station and open fire with high-velocity weapons was not given the same weight. I had been guilty of that way of thinking myself for many years. But experience had changed all that.

Nonetheless, the first-hand account of what had happened at Loughgall all those years ago gave rise to conflicting emotions for me. Without doubt, there was anger at the way the IRA had acted in targeting Loughgall in the first place. But likewise, nothing could justify how the SAS, aided by the Det, had tackled the operation.

George's account left me in no doubt that arrests would have been possible and that the savagery of the assault was way over the top. I knew that much of the grief and heartache experienced by the families of the eight men would have been due to the merciless manner in which they had died. My personal connection to the ambush, Seamus Donnelly, was just nineteen years old at the time. Had he been arrested on that day instead of being gunned down, he would later have been released under the Good Friday Agreement and perhaps, like others, had the opportunity of a fresh start and a non-violent life.

'Yes, politically it was a fuck-up,' George admitted. 'We did more for IRA recruitment than anything they could have done themselves. The funerals were viewed worldwide and worse still the heavy RUC presence at them made the whole thing look even more sinister. Public opinion swung against us. We did learn from it, though: now we go for the arrest every time, or almost every time.'

15 DEADLY DILEMMA

I hope this provides some answers for her.

*

'Seán Tech to the briefing room!'

By July 2002, nine months into the job, I had come to hate those six words squawking from the speaker in the tech bay. Without exception they meant my workload was about to get even heavier.

I pulled myself out from beneath the vehicle I was working on. It was fully stripped down to its shell but still not even halfway through its full fit-out. As always, the operator, in this case Stephen – an SBS soldier on attachment at North Det – wanted it back as quickly as possible so that he could escape from the shit duties he had been given while the vehicle was out of action. He wanted to get back out 'on the ground'.

He'd have to wait now, though. There was something going down. The Det had been a hive of activity since early morning. My radio monitoring the net was going non-stop: 'Alpha, Golf check on three,' and so on, with the operators doing vehicle and body radio checks for 'dead' spots around Derry, Strabane and down towards the border.

Two of the operators, Baz and Damien, had been asking for urgent technical once-overs and if I had any new covert cameras that I could fit for them. Something big was brewing, obviously, but we support staff would be told only when Colin Opso was ready.

I cleaned myself up a bit, gave Alan the heads-up and made my way over to the Spanner's bay. One of them was busy under a vehicle while, as I'd guessed, Jim was getting cleaned up himself. He'd had the tannoy call too, and he and I always hooked up prior to a briefing to make sure we were on the same page. While our job as techs and spanners was to ensure all the operator and surveillance vehicles were fully operational, we also managed the strategy for handling the boss! We never gave Colin the full picture, keeping an ace or two up our sleeves at all times because we knew that no matter what you offered him at the initial briefing, he always wanted more. After a quick discussion, we checked in our mobile phones and pagers at the front desk of the operations building, and entered the briefing room.

It was packed, the entire Det on a leave ban and in full op mode. (Clearly the intelligence on this one was very good. It must have been ELINT or Electronic Intelligence). Intelligence briefing now finished, the head of each of the support staff departments was now present. That included me, albeit unofficially. I hadn't been formally appointed head of tech, but I had built up a relationship with Colin (and his operators) over the previous nine months that amounted to the same thing. I had huge respect for Colin, realising that he had probably forgotten more about covert surveillance than I would ever know. In turn, he appreciated the fact that I had worked my ass off to turn things around in the technical department. It went from being so bad that the operators couldn't rely on their kit or the technology, to something that everyone knew they could bet the house on, and that helped the Det do its job. So, even though Alan outranked me and was a longer time at North Det, it was me who was called to the operations room every time.

'Okay, lads, new operation. Everything focused on this until it finishes out,' Colin announced in his Manchester accent and nasal tones. 'What state are we in?' Each of the heads gave a rundown of the state of his department. We heard about the ammunition from Ali DQ, the radio network from Jamie Pronto, photography from Will Brownie, and mechanics from Jim Spanner. He made sure Colin knew that the operators were wrecking cars quicker than he could repair them. Colin already knew all this, as we each gave him a written report every morning, but he still liked to hear it straight from the horse's mouth at briefings.

For my report, I didn't even have to think. By now I knew every vehicle at North Det from a surveillance perspective, their contents and their operational status. I had also committed to memory the location of every camera that North Det had control of, and the targets they covered. 'I've got a vehicle in the bay that I can have ready to go in a few days with a push: everyone else is good to go. All the specialist vehicles are fully operational. There are two cameras down at Rosemount and Strand Road, but "Cameras" are waiting on spares before we can sort them out. I've got some extra covert cameras on the shelf, but the lads have already been in this morning to book those.'

'How many spare vehicles do we have?' Colin asked, generating a few giggles around the room. Everyone in the room knew that I would hold back on what I really had available, just as they knew he would ask for more.

'Two spare, with a full surveillance fit needed for one before it's ready,' I answered, trying not to laugh myself.

Colin didn't seem to notice, and grunted back, 'Not good enough. I want six, minimum, and I want those cameras back up and running, too. If you need me to make any calls to get help from HQ, tell me.' This was the kind of thing Jim and I had expected, and we had five vehicles back in the covert hanger and enough kit for three fit-outs. I winked over at Jim and got a cheeky grin in return.

I suggested bastardising some kit from East and South

Dets to get those cameras up and running, One thing Colin liked more than North Det being fully operational was when it involved robbing one of the other Dets of kit.

'Do it!' was his reply.

The operation to hand was around a Derry city- and Strabane-based Real IRA cell. The cell was led by a Republican figure who had been on the fringes of the PIRA but had moved to the dissident movement where he could be a bigger fish in a much smaller pond. He'd previously had a reputation for being nothing but a thug and, without doubting that, we now honoured him with a North Det 'Charlie One' status for the first time, as the primary target of this surveillance operation.

Central to the operation was a white Vauxhall Cavalier, thought, from ELINT to be the proposed transport vehicle for an IED that was to be planted somewhere in North Det's area. Only the where and when were unknown. Our first job was to get a tracking device on the vehicle. This would free up the operators to focus on the people. The planting was scheduled for the Sunday-night/early Monday-morning period always favoured by operators for covert work, when the streets are at their quietest and most of the world is deeply asleep. To achieve the best surveillance results, the method we used involved temporarily stealing the target car, hopefully without anyone noticing, and then leaving an identical car with the same number plates in its place while the tracking device was embedded in the original car. If anyone did notice the car being stolen, we would simply burn it out somewhere to make it look like just another car theft, which were two a penny in Northern Ireland.

At about 0300, with the streets of Derry entirely dead, in one smooth, flowing movement of operators dressed in normal civilian clothing, and communicating with just clicks on the radio network, one white Vauxhall Cavalier parked on a driveway in Derry was unlocked, opened and rolled silently away while another was rolled into its place. Within an hour the dance was repeated and we all went home to bed.

Next morning, Gill, our liaison officer with TCG, was dispatched to their compound on the other side of the airfield. Linked into the Dets radio network from there (as no TCG personnel were ever allowed access to our communications or intelligence) she was then able to help direct PSNI patrols around Det operations and so avoid any so-called 'blue on blue incidents' which had occurred in the past.

From then on, everyone was flat out with the usual tactics. We were 'turning over' our vehicles like hot cakes, some just needing their number plates changed, while others were swapped out entirely when the operators sensed that they might have been compromised while tailing targets. The operation was following a typical pattern: surveillance was twenty-four hours a day, with operators working in shifts and resting up at their temporary base at Clooney near the city. Occasionally they would get back to Ballykelly for a shower and a decent feed but it was hard going and I didn't envy them.

The Cavalier was moved a few times, the Real IRA cell doing their best to counteract what they knew of the State's surveillance tactics. Eventually they even moved it across the border into the Republic, believing it couldn't be tracked there. They were wrong. Meanwhile, the players' targets remained under constant surveillance for about two weeks.

Then, suddenly, on 31 July, 'Standby! Standby!' echoed around the compound, which meant get your arse in gear, something was stirring. There was a buzz about the place as everyone got ready. It was late afternoon and most of us were busy on routine stuff in our own workshops. We dropped everything and went with the spooks and operators to the operations room. I was there in case something went wrong with any of the surveillance kit at the last minute. The room was fully manned, with Colin at the wall of monitors, headset on, controlling the surveillance cameras and barking orders to the operators already on the ground. The rest of the operators were dispatched, though not before checking their weapons, including SIG sauer 9mm pistols, MP5 sub-machine guns, HK53 assault rifles and pump-action shotguns – more than enough to deal with any trouble they might run into.

'Seán, get your gear and head to the FMB [Forward Mounting Base] at Clooney. I want everyone on the ground. Any faults, deal with them there.' I loaded up the tech vehicle with some spares, my tools and rigger's kit, and at the armoury I got my own SIG sauer pistol, three loaded magazines and a HK53 complete with two full magazines. As I drove out of the compound, I inserted my covert earpiece and made my own radio checks: 'Alpha, Tuner check on three', 'Tuner' being my very apt call sign. 'Lima Charlie, Tuner'.

The Cavalier was on the move from the Republic across the border and into Derry. We tracked it moving around the city, stopping a few times, no doubt as counter-surveillance measures. The operators at the Det, especially the ones who had served a long time at North, had a grudging respect for PIRA volunteers, their discipline and training. By comparison, the dissidents were a bunch of criminal thugs, and there was not much respect for them. (The new breed of Republicans, the 'Dissidents', as they liked to be known, were all about image. Image, money and power, hidden behind the guise of the Republican tradition. The grudging respect the operators had for the old guard, the Provisionals, did not apply to this group of thugs.) But they only needed to get lucky once, so there was no complacency in how we handled ourselves.

Soon the car stopped and pulled in off the road where it

was joined by another vehicle. A number of men, including our Charlie One, emerged. The vehicles were boot to boot and the men crowded around in between as if trying to block something from view. They then split into two groups, one driving north towards Ballykelly with Charlie One now on board and the other, the Cavalier, heading south-east through Co. Derry towards Armagh. Decision time: should we stick with the Cavalier or flip to the other vehicle carrying Charlie One? All the intelligence told us the white Cavalier would be carrying the explosives, so Colin made the call to stick with it. Now heading towards the border, with the operators following discreetly, it didn't stop at its previous hide but instead kept on heading south-east, all the way into Co. Louth. This was unexpected and Colin was worried. He directed all resources, including the PSNI through Gill, to track down the second vehicle and Charlie One. We scoured the city and the surrounding areas down as far as Strabane, checking all the usual haunts, but it was the early hours of the next morning (Thursday, 1 August) before Charlie One was found back home in Strabane. While everyone breathed a sigh of relief at this, it was a short one.

Later we heard that a civilian worker and former UDR soldier, David Caldwell, picked up a lunchbox as he arrived for work at Caw Camp Territorial Army centre on the Limavady Road. The box contained a booby-trapped IED and exploded, mortally injuring Caldwell. He died at Altnagelvin Hospital. Intelligence later gathered by North would show that the lunchbox had been transferred from the white Vauxhall into the second vehicle. From there it was taken sometime in the early hours of the morning and planted in Caw camp. North had been wrong-footed.

The mood on the Det that morning was one of anger, not just at the death of David Caldwell, a father of four, but at ourselves for having failed the man. The debriefing that followed was frank and surgical. What had gone wrong, we asked ourselves. Where could we have done better, we debated. That night was spent in the Det bar, normal practice after an operation was concluded, but instead of the usual celebrations, it was more a case of drowning sorrows and licking wounds. As we sat and chatted in small groups, we went over things and in a few cases tempers flared up in disagreement. That was normal, too: the tension finding a release.

It's been fourteen years since the murder of David Caldwell and his family are still asking for a full enquiry. As for Charlie One on that operation, he remains committed to the Republican movement. The white Vauxhall Cavalier was found burned out in a field in Co. Louth, the tracking device still working even after it had been torched. I know it was there because I checked on it on one of my trips home later that year.

Until now, no one had any knowledge of North Det's involvement in the incident. David Caldwell's daughter, Gillian McFaul, has been looking for answers ever since that day. I hope this provides some.

16 HARVEY STREET

They had moved in too quickly, and ended up making a complete balls of what should have been a straightforward finish to a somewhat chaotic surveillance operation. Months of work had gone into the operation, but despite the arrests made and the recovery of a Mark 16 mortar, launch tube and firing pack, along with other bomb-making items, those arrested would sidestep the law and get away scot-free.

I had been at North Det now for a year and was well used to the unpredictable working hours, heavy workload and the claustrophobic nature of being confined to the secure compound at Ballykelly. I made the most of my time at the Det, learning new skills from the operators and SAS/SBS lads who were posted there. I went to the firing ranges as often as possible; they were a lot more fun than range days at a normal green army unit. The lads ran me through scenarios that I had never encountered before and I became proficient in all manner of weapons. I sparred in the boxing ring whenever there was some downtime.

That said, things were beginning to change at North Det and not necessarily for the better. We now had a new operations officer, Glenn Opso, and a whole new intake of operators fresh from training. They were replacing many of those I had become good friends with, and it was inevitable that I would compare the new with the old in favour of my old mates.

All the intelligence for the operation had come from Harvey Street, the location that was under the most intense surveillance since long before I arrived at North Det and would, I guessed, remain so long after I had left. It took me a while to learn why Colin had put so much emphasis on it in terms of resources, even if meant sacrifices had to made elsewhere. As usual, it was in the Det bar that all was revealed and this time by Colin himself before he left North Det.

Harvey Street was the jewel in North Det's crown; it had yielded a wealth of intelligence since it was first monitored. Many of the people seen coming and going had proven to be major players in the Republican movement and they would give North Det many arrests. It was also the location of a major IRA arms cache, control over which – with the recent rise of the dissidents –was changing hands quicker than we could keep up with. Its fate all came down to one man, the IRA quartermaster in control of the cache. He didn't seem to know which group to side with, veering from the Real IRA to the Continuity IRA (CIRA), and sometimes taking a middle ground. North Det's greatest fear was that the cache would be moved and broken up, making it much more difficult to keep under surveillance, especially if an attempt was made to move it over the border. I could see the need for the constant surveillance. But there was a twist in the tale of Harvey Street.

Charlie One was Anthony Thomas Friel from Elmwood Terrace in Derry's Bogside. A Mark 16 mortar and other items were known to be located in a garage on Tryconnell Street at the rear of the target house. Friel had been traced from connections with nearby Harvey Street and was now subject to all the surveillance assets that North Det had at its disposal. Listening devices had been planted and surveillance cameras redeployed to put the house and garage under 24/7 surveillance. Friel himself had a constant tail on him too as he went about his business. His skills in counter-surveillance were lacking in the extreme.

It was about two days before the operation came to a conclusion when Matt Op popped his head into the tech bay and tossed me a mobile phone: 'I need everything off it and back to me in ten minutes, and don't forget to wipe your fingerprints before you give it back!' This one had obviously been lifted from Charlie One's car or house, I surmised, and needed to be returned as soon as possible.

One of the tools we had was a 'mobile phone forcer', used to download all the information, text messages, phone logs and picture messages from a mobile phone, even the deleted stuff. The paramilitaries had yet to fully discover the vulnerabilities of using mobile phones, so I was able to get a wealth of information from the device. The phone was returned to Charlie One in no time, and he was none the wiser. We learned from the downloads that an attack using the Mark 16 mortar was imminent.

Surveillance was to be upped over the weekend, and then, on Monday, 28 October, once Friel was in possession of the mortar, an arrest was to be made. Monday morning was chosen to ensure that there was plenty of traffic about and that the operator and RCG (Regional Co-ordination Group) vehicles could approach the target without rousing too much attention. Glenn, the new operations officer, made the decision that the PSNI RCG team would make the arrest. That turned out to be a mistake.

The two overt-surveillance cameras located at the Masonic mast that would normally cover the Bogside area of the city were not able to give a good enough view of Elmwood Street and so a specialist surveillance vehicle had to be deployed. Glenn chose to deploy one of our best, capable of transmitting images back to the Det from almost anywhere in the city. I fully agreed with the idea.

However, the proximity of the target to the Bogside Inn,

a staunchly Republican bar, and its location in the middle of the IRA heartland of the Bogside, meant that there would be few opportunities to insert the vehicle. On Sunday morning, I sat in the operations room waiting for it to be put in place so I could run the cameras through their final checks before handing over to Glenn. Mike, one of the new operators, drove the vehicle into position but didn't follow normal procedure. He armed the alarm system and engaged the engine cut-off switch and left the vehicle before letting me check the cameras from the operations room. It turned out he had parked too far back and left us with no view of the target.

Sending Mike back to the car to move it would arouse too much suspicion. It would have to be extracted and another vehicle inserted in its place. Mike was in for a bollocking when he got back.

'Sorry, Seán, but I'll need the surveillance kit transferred into one of the spare cars and it needs to be back in place tonight before we kick the doors in tomorrow morning.' Glenn was genuinely apologetic.

Mike pulled the vehicle into one of spaces in the tech bay about an hour later. I had an Opel Corsa in the other bay, ready to start fitting it out with the surveillance cameras, alarm and radio equipment.

'Shit, Seán, I'm sorry, mate, I'll give you a hand stripping it out.'

He was furious with himself and I had no intention of making him feel any worse.

'You're alright, Mike, get back out on the ground, I'll manage.'

I started to strip the kit and was working on it well into Sunday night before I was near getting it finished. Then the tannoy system sounded, summoning me to the operations room. Glenn wanted to be clear on the best position for the vehicle so he could get a blocking car in there to reserve the space. I hadn't yet left the workshop when Simon OC arrived over to give a hand. I was fitting the specialised surveillance antenna to the roof of the Corsa, a delicate enough task and one I didn't want him messing around with. Simon wasn't the most gifted with his hands. He was, however, the OC. I asked him to start refitting the seats, though I knew I'd redo them myself when I got back.

Even though I was back from the operations room within twenty minutes, Simon had managed in that time to totally screw up my fit-out. He had taken it upon himself to try to fit the antenna, but cut too big a hole in the roof for the cable. His solution was to reverse the direction of the antenna, with the result that it now looked like a fucking unicorn with the antenna pointing forwards instead of to the rear! Chances of it standing out: 100 per cent.

Glenn exploded at Simon: 'What the fuck have you done? I can't deploy that; it will stand out a mile.' He looked over at me: 'Can we get another vehicle fitted in time Seán?' The look on my face gave him his answer. 'Okay, we'll have to send it out as it is and hope that it goes unnoticed. Once this job is over, Seán, scrap that vehicle. I never want to see it again.' Glenn stormed out of the tech bay closely followed by Simon, who had the appearance of a child caught stealing candy.

At around 0200 the Corsa was ready to be inserted, this time by Sharon Op. I sat in the operations room, as before, ready to test the cameras. As we watched the car pass the Bogside Inn on the overwatch cameras on the Masonic mast, both Glenn and I mumbled, 'Oh fuck!' It looked even worse as it travelled the quiet streets of Derry than it had in the tech bay. I was certain that the vehicle and therefore the entire operation would be compromised, but the car was soon in place without a hitch.

All the operators were withdrawn until later that morning when the Bogside would come back to life.

Everyone stayed at Clooney Barracks, awaiting Glenn 's order to re-enter the city. I was on standby in case the cameras failed, for any reason, and to watch the finale to this operation. It had, after all, been a complete pain in the arse for everyone involved.

Eventually, Charlie One left the house on Elmwood Street that morning. He had previously been seen meeting a number of other known dissidents, in what was thought to be a final meeting in preparation for the attack on the PSNI. As he was returning to the house, Glenn ordered the operators to close in and tighten the net, while the PSNI patrols, through Gill LO, moved into the area to make the arrest once Glenn had given the order. He had a full view of the house from the cameras in the Corsa and we watched Charlie One move along the street and into the house. 'Standby! Standby!' Glenn called over the net.

Suddenly, the PSNI patrols had a Go! Go! Go! Order from the TCG Opso and moved into Elmwood Street. The order should have come from Glenn and no one else. They sealed the area off, smashed in the doors and entered the house, while Glenn sat there screaming down the net at Gill, 'What the hell are they doing?' Gill was as bewildered as we were. Friel was still in the house, nowhere near the garage where we knew the Mark 16 mortar to be. The plan had been to move in only once he was in the garage, giving concrete evidence that he was in possession of the device. Now they had Charlie One and the weapons but no way of linking the two. What should have been a certain conviction was now doubtful, unless forensics could do so later, not always reliable in cases like these, as had been shown in the past.

The debriefing was long and painful. All the screw-ups were analysed in minute detail and while quite a few of the operators took some heat, the PSNI got most of the blame. And whatever about Charlie One, we had another weapon off the streets at least, and so celebrated that smaller victory in our usual flamboyant style.

Later, Friel's defence lawyer did indeed claim that Friel never used the garage, that it was unlocked and could therefore have been used by anyone to store the items, that the mortar was not in a usable state, and that there was no forensic evidence against his client.

Harvey Street still had one more secret to yield in connection with an IRA quartermaster, and it removed whatever little respect I still had for the Republican cause and those still fighting for it.

17 TOUT

Charlie One was a former Republican prisoner, convicted of possession of AKM assault rifles and ammunition with intent to endanger life. A 'family man' from Derry, he had been part of the Republican movement from an early age. After the signing of the Good Friday Agreement had, ironically, given him his freedom, he continued his involvement in the armed struggle with the Real IRA. He teamed up with a man who became one of the most dangerous and unpredictable dissident Real IRA members, and together they were responsible for some of the most brutal terrorist attacks in Northern Ireland. Once again, it was Harvey Street – the gift that kept on giving – that had led North Det to this Charlie One: its most puzzling.

*

On two previous occasions during my time at North Det this particular Charlie One had been followed to a weapons cache within our AOR. Both operations had involved months of surveillance, hundreds of man-hours and the deployment of some of JCU-NI's most valuable surveillance assets, yet Charlie One remained a free man. Not only free, but able to continue with his role as a quartermaster within the dissident Republican movement.

It was the manner in which Charlie One was allowed to walk away each time that raised the suspicions of North Det personnel. Both operations had gone right down to the wire: Charlie One had actually been in the weapons hide and in possession of either weapons or explosive substances: usually more than enough for us to nail our target! And yet we didn't. Strangely, on both occasions the JCU-NI HQ at Lisburn had asked to be kept informed of the operation as it proceeded. They were normally only briefed before and after.

In one of the operations, as the operators tailed Charlie One into the weapons hide, they heard the familiar 'Standby! Standby!' order from the team at Ballykelly. Adrenaline flowing, they awaited the 'Go, Go! Go!' order. But it never came. Instead, the operations officer directed them to stand down, having been told to do so by JCU-NI HQ in Lisburn. During the debriefing no explanation was given ... because the operations officer didn't have one. Soldiers are used to things not making sense, so the operators just shrugged it off.

When it happened a second time, though, intense speculation began. One possible explanation was that this Charlie One was seen as being able to lead the unit to more targets. However, such a scenario would usually be communicated by HQ at the very beginning of an operation, to save on resources. No one had an explanation.

Our suspicions resurfaced some six months later when we were presented with another golden opportunity to nab him red-handed. Would it be another massive waste of time and effort with no explanation? Would North Det's sense of control be undermined again?

*

The weapons cache was once more located in the Republican heartland of the Bogside in Derry. The red-brick terraced house containing the weapons was just like the hundreds of others in the area, but its contents were far more lethal.

Surveillance for the operators was very difficult here: the

proximity of the cache to the Republican watering hole of the Bogside Inn and the vigilance of the local population made moving around the area, either in their vehicles or on foot, a difficult and risky task. No listening or tracking devices were deployed on the premises in this instance due – we were told – to the risk of compromise. There was some doubt about this explanation as we had inserted them in far riskier circumstances before.

Instead, it was the camera network we relied on. The two overt-surveillance cameras mounted on the mast at Masonic gave a great view of both the hide and the surrounding streets. It was effectively impossible to visit the cache without being seen by North Det at Ballykelly. Charlie One lived within a few streets of the weapons cache and while he was careful about his approaches, it made little difference. He would take elaborate routes into the city before returning to the Bogside, all the while under the watchful eye of North Det's surveillance cameras and operators. He had been responsible for leading North Det to a number of other, lower-ranking Republican dissidents but it was the quartermaster himself that North Det wanted.

I wouldn't like to say that the operators lacked enthusiasm, but there definitely wasn't the same buzz of excitement in the briefing room that I would have expected for an operation of this scale. Covert surveillance is such a difficult task at the best of times, with results so difficult to produce that when a target is so casually let slip, not once but twice, it is difficult to motivate people to take on a third operation. Glenn Opso had to do just that.

'You all know "Charlie One" well, so I won't go through the background again. Suffice to say, we want him in bracelets by the end of this operation.'

A call came from the back of the room: 'We wanted him in cuffs the last two times, as well.' Baz Op's jibe was met with a chorus of cheers and laughter from the rest of the room.

'Fair point, but we treat this operation like any other, so I expect the best from everyone.' Despite their misgivings, I knew there was no question but that they would give 100 per cent: they were too well trained for anything else.

Glenn continued, 'The plan is to use as many of the surveillance cameras and specialist vehicles as possible and use the operator cars as rolling surveillance on both the target house and Charlie One. We'll wait until the next time Charlie One makes a mid-week, night-time visit to the hide to strike. That should make surveillance easier and the takedown safer. We'll allow Charlie One a few minutes on-site to get himself good and comfortable, then move in. We will be making the entry ourselves this time, supported by RCG.'

There were no questions about why Glenn wasn't letting RCG go in first, considering their performance at our last outing. Glenn then went round each of the departments as normal.

'Seán, take Mark Tech to Rosemount and mount another camera there. I want it pointing straight at the front door of the hide and it stays there until this one is finished.'

Mark Tech was my new colleague, only just arrived at North Det as Alan Tech's replacement. He was a good-humoured Scottish lad who had spent much of his career to date in Germany. By comparison with Alan, Mark was very keen and extremely capable.

I decided not to wait another night but to head to Rosemount there and then to mount the camera and direct it at the door. Mark and I loaded up the tech vehicle, got our weapons from the armoury and headed for Derry. Along the way we carried out our normal radio checks to the operations room, letting them know our progress towards the city. Mark was nervous.

'Are the operators going to be out on the ground to cover us?' he asked, as casually as he could.

'Not tonight, mate, but we'll be fine. It's always quiet on a Monday night in the city and the lads stationed at Rosemount are on the ball. We'll be in and out in no time.'

We were trained to always vary our route when entering the city: if someone has managed to tag you, you don't want to make it easy for them to mount an ambush. The tech vehicle was also changed on a regular basis, and by now I never worried too much about moving around, confident in my own abilities to both talk and shoot my way out of a situation.

We arrived at Rosemount at about 0100. It was bitterly cold, with a surprisingly icy wind blowing for the time of year: a rigger's nightmare. We unloaded the vehicle and squeezed the camera, a smaller covert one, into a backpack. It still weighed over 20kg and while difficult to climb the mast with, it was easier than setting up a series of pulleys and ropes, which took more time than I wanted to spend on-site. I started up the ladder, carrying the camera. Mark was to follow after with the bag load of tools, clamps and brackets needed to attach the camera to the mast. When I got to the position where I wanted to mount the camera I unloaded it and waited for Mark. I didn't really notice the time going by but it must have been over twenty minutes and there was still no sign of him. I had no choice: leaving the camera, I started back down the ladder. Halfway down I found Mark holding on to the ladder for dear life, frozen with fear.

'You all right, mate?'

He was pale and shivering, and gave no response. I needed to get the kit off his back first before somehow manoeuvring him down from the mast. I didn't want to spook him any further, so instead of getting him to let go of the ladder and slip off the pack, I took a knife from my tool belt and cut the straps. I tossed the backpack to the ground where it landed with an almighty clatter. I hoped there was no one around: we were a pair of sitting ducks at that moment. Prising Mark's hands from the ladder, taking one rung at a time, we reached the ground almost an hour later. I put him into the car to get warm and headed back up the ladder: I still had a camera to rig and no urge to come back the next night. Rigging a camera on your own is difficult, but there's nothing like the approach of dawn to speed you up, and so just as the sun was rising we pulled out of the gates of Rosemount to make our way back to Ballykelly.

Now that all the drama was over, I had a question: 'How the hell did you pass your riggers course?'

Mark's answer was simpler than I expected: 'I haven't taken it yet.'

What was I to do? Glenn needed to know that he had a technician that couldn't rig, but there was no way Mark would pass the course. If he didn't pass his course there'd be no place for him at Cameras or Radios; he would be 'returned to unit'. I decided I'd wait until this operation was over before taking action: I needed whatever support I could get for an operation of this size.

It was two weeks later that the operation came to a climax. During that time, both Mark and I worked around the clock keeping the fleet on the road. Aside from the inability to rig, he was a great technician.

Sharon Op called in a sighting as she drove past the house: 'Charlie One is Foxtrot [on foot] towards the Bogside Inn.' Mark was resting and I was alone in the tech bay, listening to the radio net while catching up on paperwork (something I found surprisingly therapeutic). In the operations room Glenn would, I knew, be moving the cameras into position to follow Charlie One. This was his usual habit: into his local for a few pints, where those who knew of his time spent in prison for the cause would show him the respect he believed he deserved. A couple of hours later, though, Charlie One left the Bogside Inn and didn't head home as normal. Instead, he began to take a walk around the streets of the Bogside. Slowly and cautiously, he began to get closer and closer to the house where the weapons cache was. Glenn was choreographing the operators around the area; where the operators lost sight, the specialist surveillance vehicles with their hidden cameras enabled Glenn to pick him up. He was walking into a perfectly and patiently laid trap.

He made his way to the target street, stopping outside the house for a few seconds to look around before quickly letting himself in.

Glenn's plan was for three vehicles, 'two-up' (i.e. two people in each), to pull up outside the house. The first pair would smash in the door, while the other two pairs would pile in and make the arrest. All would be wearing luminous yellow hats identifying them as police, not military. They knew the layout well, the plans for the house having been obtained weeks before. The rest of the operators would be circling around the area, ready to provide support if needed. At the same time RCG would move in with their armoured Landrovers and seal off the area. They would take over from the operators once Charlie One was subdued, and North Det would once more disappear into the night.

'Standby! Standby!' came the order over the net. I could imagine the operators cocking their weapons in preparation for the entry, the adrenalin building as they mentally went through their checklist, ensuring they hadn't overlooked anything. The tension was high for everyone, including me, at the prospect of finally getting to take this bastard down. The seconds ticked away. The thought occurred to me that the operators might jump the gun before anyone could stop them, but they waited patiently as per their training.

Then it came. 'All call signs, stand down! Stand down! Return to base!' I could hear the disappointment in Glenn's voice, and knew he was gutted. He may have been gutted but the rest of the team was livid. The language bouncing around the radio net was worse than I'd ever heard, but there was nothing to be done about it. Within twenty minutes the operators had returned to the Det and went for the debriefing. The rest of us, after weeks of hard work, made our way to the bar. There was no attempt by the operators to hide their anger as they joined us later. The speculation was now rife that Charlie One was a 'tout'. Even Glenn had to agree that was the only explanation. There could be no other reason that he would be allowed off the hook on so many occasions. He wasn't leading North Det to anything better, so it must be someone else getting the benefits: whoever his handlers were. We drank well into the following morning, with the excuse that we needed to wipe this Charlie One from our minds and make ourselves ready for the next operation. But the tale of this Charlie One wasn't yet over.

About a month later, North Det was holding its annual sports day. There was an open invitation to all JCU-NI personnel to attend and all the other Dets, including HQ, would send anyone not on duty for the glorified piss-up. With so many strangers around, the operations building, tech bays and anywhere else containing sensitive information were locked up and the main focus was kept to the bar area. We started at lunchtime with a BBQ and the drinking began then. By early nightfall everyone was well on their way to being drunk. One of those attending was recognised by one of the operators as an agent handler, having encountered him on the training course at Hereford. He joined our little group and inevitably the subject of Charlie One came up. Alcohol being the biggest scourge of British army intelligence, this guy confirmed what we had all suspected: 'Yeah, he sings like a canary, that guy. Why do you think that you weren't allowed to put a listening device into any of the hides? We didn't want you guys overhearing anything. We have him just where we want him.'

Tony Op, always sceptical, said, 'We've never seen him meet with anyone that we haven't been able to ID, so how is he getting the information to you?'

'We have our own ways of getting information back from him. He's not the only one in your AOR, either, you know.' The names he shared with us nearly sobered me up, I was so surprised: two well-known Sinn Féin politicians were providing information to British Intelligence and had been for years.

Charlie One later left Derry, with, many at the Det believed, the help of British Intelligence, but not before he had been part of a number of other terrorist attacks. How much information he had provided for his freedom, we'll probably never know. Each time I see the two MLAs on television I cringe as they spout on about their Republican ideals, knowing full well that they had sold them out long ago, if they ever really existed.

As for Mark, fortunately he got over his fear of heights and remained at North Det.

18 THE BOOK

Critical to the successful insertion of a covert-surveillance device to any premises or vehicle is what is known as 'The Book'. As soon as the decision is made to conduct such an operation, The Book is begun for that specific operation.

The Book contains every single detail of intelligence that is gathered in the build-up to the insertion. It starts with background information on the target themselves and on their family members. Then every move they make is logged. When each of them gets up in the morning, when they go to bed, what time they leave the house and return, any other patterns that might emerge in their movements. Visitors to the house, their identities, how long they stayed; family pets – especially dogs, what time the pets were walked or let out; the premises itself, the exact position of curtains and blinds, the times they were opened and closed, when the lights in each room were turned on and off, what type of lock was on the doors, front and back. Sketches would be made of the locks and the type of keys required to open them; the alarm system, the master code to bypass that type of alarm system; people who walked or drove by the house or hung around the vicinity regularly.

The depth of information that was collated 24/7 and added to The Book was staggering. It formed an extensive insight into the target's life and was essential for the successful execution of any operation on a target. Whoever would have imagined that The Book would end up being the one thing that ruined an operation.

*

The newspaper headlines said it all.

'*Sinn Féin man says British Intelligence broke into his house*'

'*British Intelligence blamed for covert break-ins*'

and so on.

The fallout at North Det was instantaneous; the two operators involved were summoned immediately to JCU-NI Headquarters in Lisburn, and a helicopter was sent for them. There would be no stonewalling, it seemed; someone was for the chop. The issue wasn't that North Det had carried out such an operation. The problem was that we had been caught.

The Sinn Féin propaganda machine was now in full flow, and it was something to be in awe of. What was most frustrating for us was the fact that none of this might have come about: in all but one respect, it had been a perfectly executed operation.

Charlie One was Raymond McCartney, a former hunger striker in 1980, OC for the IRA prisoners in the Maze, and a senior Sinn Féin member in Derry. He had been under regular surveillance by North Det for a long time. That routine surveillance had changed to 24/7 in recent times, and the objective of this operation was simply to plant a number of listening devices in his home. These would then be monitored continuously by personnel from 2 SCT, based in Moscow camp in Belfast. This type of surveillance was hard to beat in that no matter how well trained a target was in counter-surveillance, once in the comfort of their own home, they invariably slipped up at some stage and blurted out something useful.

With Glenn Opso now in charge, I saw huge contrasts between his style of command and Colin's. Colin had been very proactive in every aspect of North's operations. He pushed the boundaries to their very limit and often well beyond. He was unwilling to accept anything average from any of us. Glenn, though vastly experienced in his own right, seemed happy with whatever hand was dealt him. He had a much more laid-back approach and while that was a bonus for us as technicians, it wasn't always the best in terms of managing operators and their differences.

For every operation of this scale, there was a number one and a number two operator in charge on the ground. Unfortunately, the gulf between the number one and number two for this job couldn't have been greater, and Glenn as Opso had failed to resolve it. Frank Op, the number one, had recently taken over as Det sergeant major (DSM). He was very experienced, with multiple tours under his belt at a number of the JCU-NI Dets over the years. At the other end of the scale, Keith, number two, was on his first tour with the Det, having only recently passed the gruelling six-month JCU-NI selection and training course in Wales. He was now OC for North Det, replacing Simon. This OC position was only a figurehead one, as the Opso was, in effect, in charge, but it was a big deal in Keith's eyes. This was his first operation after his six-week orientation phase, and he was really up for it, keen to show what he could do. He had been in with me several times in the lead-up, picking my brains for anything new he could get for the job. I could see he was a guy that had great potential in the clandestine world in which we operated, assuming Lady Luck was on his side.

The day arrived: the first Saturday in June. The window of opportunity was very small as McCartney and his family would return the next day: one night for the operators to complete the insertion and confirm the device was fully operational. It was not an optimum night for such a task, what with people spilling out of pubs, clubs and parties throughout the city, but North Det had an array of options to overcome this problem. As before, we would use the vast network of overt-surveillance cameras dotted around the city to help us through. And, on this occasion, we would call on one other major ally.

From time to time, the Det borrowed specialist personnel from MI5, or 'Box' as they were known within the trade. One such person, a regular at North Det, was 'Bill', which was obviously not his real name, but was all the information we were ever given about him. A middle-aged man, he would arrive through Belfast International Airport, complete with his angling gear, which was part of his cover for his regular visits to Northern Ireland. Bill had a very special talent: the ability to defeat almost any electronic security system that was on the market, and many that weren't.

McCartney's house had already been surveyed for an alarm system, of course, and the details forwarded to Box. But experience had shown that many of our targets had additional security systems installed that weren't immediately apparent. It was only on entering some premises that these would be discovered, or worse: wouldn't be discovered at all. That was where Bill came in, with his impressive ability to sniff out a previously unidentified system and neutralise it. (It was a skill I would learn myself later and put to good use when I left the ranks of the British army.)

Once the briefing finished that Saturday, I took my regular position floating between the operations room and the front desk. From there I could monitor the radio and cameras network from a technical perspective, freeing up space in the operations room.

With McCartney and his family now confirmed, via a tracking device either located on his person or car, to be at their holiday location, the operation began. It started with a six-man team of operators in their vehicles taking up various positions around the Shantallow area of Derry city, where he lived. They cautiously probed the streets leading into the area, looking for any paramilitary IVCPs that may have sprung up. These were not uncommon, especially in such IRA heartlands. They could have 'eyes' on all the streets approaching the house. The probe team, combined with the overt cameras, would give the insertion team a heads-up on anyone that might be out to rumble them. Operators in vehicles and on foot were much closer to the premises. Sharon and Jack were picked to pose as a drunken couple on their way home from a night out, stopping for a kiss and a bit of a cuddle along the street from McCartney's house. (I think Glenn had paired them on purpose, knowing she didn't like Jack. He was certainly no oil painting, either, compared to the eye candy she could have been paired with. But like the pro she was, she offered it up in the service of queen and country!)

Further down the street and propped against the wall was Will. He didn't need to do much acting, he actually looked like a wino. Despite appearances, he had eyes on the front door of the house and was in constant communication with the operations room.

The insertion team consisted of Frank, Keith, Bill and the drop-off driver, Baz. On their first two passes of the house, the team was waved on due to people being in the general area. It only took one person to raise the alarm and a big mess could be raging within a few minutes. On the third pass, Baz coasted to a stop outside the door. With his headlights off and using the cut-off switch on his dashboard, he prevented any of the car's other lights shining as he came to a halt. Once the insertion team had exited the car, Baz moved away to await the call to pick them up. This time was when the team was most vulnerable to detection; anyone passing or looking out from a neighbouring house could ruin the operation. The tension would have been too much for many people, but these guys were experts in their craft and could stay cool. Frank was first to the door, as per the plan, and used the pre-cut key to instantly open it, quickly followed inside by Bill and Keith OC.

Once inside, they set about their pre-arranged tasks. Bill checked the security system, neutralising any threat that might be posed by that. Frank and Keith started on the main job of planting the devices, a task that was not as straightforward as it might sound.

Three things were required for the successful installation of a listening device. First, it needed a permanent power source; these devices are meant to last years. Nipping in and out to change the batteries every few weeks isn't a realistic option. The solution was to link the device's rechargeable batteries to a main power supply within the premises, usually the lighting circuit, thereby ensuring it was constantly topped up. Second, it needed an aperture to the room that you were bugging, about the size of a pinhole. This allowed for a clear audio signal to be received by the device. Third, and most important, it needed a strong transmission signal. One option was a radio transmitter that would boost the signal from the device to a nearby repeater station, through JCU-NI's radio network and back to the listening post. A second option was through a GSM mobile signal, utilising the ever-increasing mobile phone network around Northern Ireland. At the time, the Det had just started using the latter. The entire device was no bigger than a cigarette lighter.

Devices planted, audio checks back to the listening post done, the team was ready for extraction. They waited for Baz to coast back to the door front, while the rest of the operators and Glenn remained vigilant. The extraction was without incident and the operators were on their way.

Back at the Det, Glenn and the spooks awaited other members of the team for the debriefing. For the rest of us, despite the hour, the celebrations had already begun. We had made our way to the bar and the drinks were flowing for another North Det success. We heard the operators' cars pulling into the covert car park in the compound, and knew they would be joining us soon enough. It was shaping up to be a great night; a couple of the lads had even pulled out guitars and begun tuning up in anticipation of what was to come.

Suddenly, Larry Spook stuck his head in and shouted, 'Everyone to the briefing room! Now!' We were perplexed. When we arrived, we weren't greeted by the smiling happy faces one would have expected following a successful job, but rather by very grim faces. I slid in beside Mandy Spook. 'What the hell is going on?' I whispered through the side of my mouth, careful not be overheard by Glenn.

'They can't find The Book. We're going to start a sweep for it now.' Her tone told me she didn't expect to find it, but I thought to myself, 'It's not that bad, it's bound to show up.'

Glenn stood at the top of the room, no sign of his usual relaxed manner on display. 'I want a sweep of all the vehicles on the compound, along with all of the rooms and workshops,' he barked. We obeyed, and repeated the sweep twice but to no avail. It was becoming apparent to me what the real fear was: that it had been left behind at McCartney house.

There was no time left to insert another team. It was daylight and he was due home that day anyway. Frank Op and Keith OC were grasping at straws, even considering asking the PSNI RCG team to conduct a raid to recover The Book. That was never going to happen, though, as JCU-NI would never let the PSNI in on such a thing. There was still a chance that it wasn't there at all, and that's what they ended up relying on.

We wouldn't know until McCartney returned home. The atmosphere at the Det meanwhile became incredibly tense, and finger-pointing began. The possibility of Frank or Keith being returned to their parent units back in the UK and under such dubious circumstances was piling the pressure on and cracks were starting to appear. They couldn't even look at each other. I hadn't experienced anything like it at North Det during my two years there, and felt that this would never have happened had Colin still been at the helm. He and Simon OC would have found a way to keep a lid on it and deal with it internally, but HQ was involved now and there was no going back. North was normally a tight-knit community that shunned outsiders and stuck together.

The operations room filled up – strictly operators and spooks, as everyone wanted to listen in on the bug through the 2 SCT net. The rest of us were giving the place a wide birth.

Charlie One arrived home in the afternoon, and our worst fears were confirmed. The Book was sitting there on his kitchen table. He knew instantly what he had in his possession.

Frank and Keith packed their bags. No time for leaving parties or farewell dinners, the handshakes exchanged said it all: they wouldn't be returning from their visit to HQ. Life at JCU-NI was unforgiving for those who screwed up. (Keith was replaced instantly with a twenty-year veteran of Det life, brought on board to 'straighten North Det out'.)

It almost goes without saying that McCartney brought in a civilian team of counter-surveillance experts to sweep his house for bugs. They didn't find a thing: a reflection of both the quality of the insertion team and the ineptitude of the team carrying out the sweep. It didn't stop McCartney putting the publicity screws on us, though, and creating a big mess for the authorities to deal with.

This wasn't North's only run-in with the McCartney family. Two years later his brother, Andrew McCartney, was having some building work done on his home and the builders found another, much older, device in the kitchen's ceiling cavity. North fucked-up again!

19 ON YOUR BIKE

It was the first time I had seen North Det move as one complete unit to another location. On many previous occasions, the operators and an assigned technician would 'forward-mount' to a temporary base for the duration of an operation, but never an entire Det.

The operations room at Ballykelly was left with a skeleton crew; itself a risky gamble should anything kick off elsewhere within our area of responsibility. Everyone, including Glenn, the spooks, Steve (the new pronto), and of course the operators, were making their way to Omagh. I was driving one of the specialist surveillance vehicles, loaded with spare equipment, with Steve as a passenger. We were discussing that morning's briefing for the operation.

'What did you make of them holding that second briefing?' Steve asked.

I had been wondering about it. After the first briefing was over, everyone, except RCG (previously TCG) and the operators, was asked to leave, and a second briefing was given. It was extremely unusual for the spooks not to be present at any briefing, as it was they who usually provided the intelligence for the briefings.

'It will come out eventually,' was all I could reply, 'it always does. But I have a feeling there will be a twist in this one. Hopefully it'll be a positive one. We've had enough screw-ups of late, haven't we?'

*

The intelligence for the operation had come from a listening device and so was considered solid. That device had been planted in the home of a well-known dissident Republican in Tyrone and was giving North Det literally volumes of first-grade intelligence. In this instance, it was to do with a planned murder of British army troops.

The target for the Real IRA active service unit were soldiers from St Lucia Barracks in Omagh. Soldiers are creatures of habit and they are as tight-fisted as they come, and the Real IRA was going to exploit both those weaknesses. Directly across the road from St Lucia Barracks was a service station that had an ATM attached to it. Despite orders to the contrary, the soldiers used to withdraw their money from there, where it was free, as opposed to within the barracks, where it cost £1.50. Soon enough, the frequency of their movements back and forth was spotted by a Real IRA intelligence cell and a decision was made to mount an attack. Their plan was simple: a vehicle would park up somewhere near enough to the army base to give a view of the gates, most likely at the Silverbirch Hotel (where I had stayed when I had come to Northern Ireland to go through the selection process to join the British army). Once a group of soldiers was seen leaving the camp and heading for the service station, the assault team would be called in. This would consist of a motorbike driver who would speed up to the ATM, and a pillion passenger who would spray the group of soldiers with automatic fire. They would then make their escape, burning out the motorbike before going across the border to the relative safety of the Republic. It sounded foolproof to them. The only problem was, they hadn't factored in the possibility of North Det having overheard all these plans being made and deciding to be present at St Lucia Barracks with some of their own plans. They were in for an unpleasant surprise.

I was last to arrive at St Lucia Barracks; it hadn't changed much since I had been there for my initial recruit interviews in 1998. But I had. My army career, especially my time at North Det, had transformed my perception of the Troubles completely. I couldn't believe how naïve about terrorism I had been all those years before. I recalled the person I had been then, deciding on a whim to join an army and see the world on the back of the generosity of Her Majesty the Queen and Her Royal Government. Now I was back to help set an ambush for a Real IRA unit.

All the operators and their vehicles were directed to an empty shed at the rear of the camp, and I followed suit. We weren't always the most welcome people in such places, looking very un-army-like and yet acting with such authority and sort of taking over. The regular army's COP was there, however, to act as liaison with the garrison troops and to provide support to North Det if needed.

First priority for the operation was to get a listening device into the farm outhouse where the stolen motorbike was being stored, a few miles west of Omagh. This would give us the exact time of the attack, thus denying the IRA unit the element of surprise. Two of the new SAS operators, Matt and Mike, were chosen by Glenn for the relatively straightforward job. I supplied a newly developed GSM device: perfect for rural locations as it needed very little power, yet had excellent signal strength. The outhouse had no power so I included a small lithium photocell battery, which just needed to be placed where it would get some sunlight.

As Glenn and the operators began planning their movements for the insertion, Steve Pronto and I set about establishing an operations room. We took over the guardhouse at the main gate to get full control of all surveillance cameras dotted around the perimeter of the camp, to which we would add our own overt- and covert-surveillance cameras in the coming hours. The guardhouse was then off limits to all non JCU-NI personnel, and despite some gripes from the regular soldiers, we had a makeshift operations room set up within a couple of hours.

The insertion operation went smoothly, using good old-fashioned soldiering skills. At about 0200 hours, Will drove the van carrying the two SAS men from the barracks and dropped them off about half a mile from the farm to make the rest of the journey on foot. They set up an observation post nearby from which they kept a close eye on the outhouse for almost an hour until they were certain that no one was around. Matt then eased himself from the hide and made his way slowly to the outhouse covered by Mike. All was quiet, and once inside Matt found a good spot to put the listening device in place. We carried out our tests and the two operators were picked up again and returned to St Lucia Barracks.

Next: set up a perimeter and get the operators in position. But something began to bother me about this plan when I became aware of it. Why did we not leave the two SAS operators in place to keep tabs on the building? Why take the risk of letting them get to the point of the attack, where people might get hurt? I decided to ask one of the operators. Damien was due out of North Det in a few weeks and in truth he had been bored by the entire experience. He was an SAS trooper, out and out, and wanted to be in the thick of the action, not skulking around gathering intelligence. He had told me in the last few days that for much of the time when he was supposed to be tailing targets, he had been parked up in his vehicle at McDonald's in the Waterside area of Derry, having a milkshake and just calling out the spots from there. I knew I would get a straight answer from him.

He had a sly grin on his face as he replied, 'This is the first job I've really wanted to be on since I got here. That second briefing back at the Det was the best news we could have been given. One of the IRA guys involved in this hit is known to have been involved in the death of an RUC officer a few years ago, but they could never get enough on him to convict him, though. This is the first real opportunity to get him for something since then, but there aren't going to be any arrests on this one, Seán. That's why we're leaving them get to the point where they're just about to open fire, that way we have just cause to engage them.

'Plus, it won't be normal soldiers at the ATM, it'll be us – more than they're bargaining for! RCG won't move in until all the shooting is done and then we'll withdraw into the barracks until all the fuss is over.'

I had always known that the operators at North Det would not shrink from a firefight if one came their way, but this was the first time I had heard them talk about an outright shoot-to- kill policy. It was already known that only the pillion passenger would be armed but the Det still planned to shoot the driver, even though he would be unarmed. Thoughts of Loughgall sprang to mind and I wondered had the Det really learned anything since then. There was no doubt that they would be able to justify their actions, but that still didn't make it right!

The Prince of Wales Own Regiment of Yorkshire were once more providing North Det with a COP, led by a guy called Neil. Neil was a career soldier and had made his way up through the ranks to make RSM and now he and a young officer were in charge of COP. I was in the guardhouse, now North Det's operations room, when the two men came in to meet with Glenn. Glenn was concentrating on setting up his surveillance cameras when the young COP officer made an announcement. 'My troops will take over the sangars and provide covering fire once the assault begins.'

Both Neil and I burst into laughter, as Glenn whipped around with a look of complete shock on his face. 'They will fucking not! Tell your troops they are weapons tight until this thing is over.' If the operators from North Det were engaged by fire from anyone they would return it, irrespective of where it came from. COP weren't well trained enough for this type of work and the young officer had yet to learn his place in this odd world of covert surveillance. The officer left with his tail between his legs. Neil apologised and assured Glenn he would be kept on a short leash. When the two men had left, Glenn looked over at me and laughed, 'Next you'll be telling me you want a go, Seán!'

It was a Friday night and we had been in Omagh for a number of days already; the longer we spent there the more obvious it was becoming to those in the barracks that something was going on. We couldn't stay there for much longer, plus our normal surveillance work was suffering with so many of us tied up down in Omagh. The operators were taking it in shifts to man the sangars, after the thought of the COP soldiers getting trigger-happy put Glenn off having them in the sangars at all. Those who weren't in the sangars were out in their vehicles, circling around Omagh.

We had also taken over the first floor of a building that was the corporals' mess for the camp, and it gave an excellent view over the service station and the ATM. Firing points were established at the windows and we made ourselves as comfortable as possible in the bar area while we awaited orders from Jim. We were sitting around chatting when a group of three soldiers came into the bar, clearly unaware that it was now occupied by Special Forces and closed for business. The look on their faces was priceless and they gazed upon the array of weapons, communications and surveillance kit strewn around.

'Sorry, lads, the bar is closed for a few days. Should be open again quite soon, we're just doing some refurbishments.' It was Baz who had spoken. When they had left, he looked around the room and asked, 'Do you think they bought my decorating story? I guess not: we should probably put a sign up on the door, then!' It broke the tension in the room. Baz was always good at that.

It was close to 2100 hours when the listening device in the outhouse sprang to life. The two men had arrived to collect the motorbike and weapon, and from there would make their way to Omagh. The operators moved into their predetermined positions. Two of the operators, dressed in normal British army uniforms, took over from the sentries at the front gate, which overlooked the service station. Those operators in the sangars ran through their weapons and communications checks. There were six operators in their vehicles moving around Omagh and now they began to move into position around the service station. In the corporals' mess the operators began to take up their firing positions for what, from their vantage point, would be a turkey shoot. The three men who had the most dangerous job in the whole operation were the three operators who would, in civilian clothing, leave the barracks through the main gate and make their way to the ATM across the road. Each man had a Kevlar vest beneath his clothing and a pistol tucked away on his person. They would have no communication with either the operations room or the other operators, and so would have no idea when the motorbike was approaching. The first they would know about it was when they heard the sound of the engine. They would be relying on the other operators to engage and neutralise the terrorists before they had an opportunity to open fire – not a position I would want to be in.

I was with Glenn in the guardhouse and he asked me to patch through the feed from the listening device to every operator, so they could respond immediately to the two men leaving the outhouse. Time was ticking by and the active service unit had still not left the outhouse. Their problem? They couldn't get the motorbike to start! It was becoming blatantly obvious that neither man had ever kick-started a motorbike before. With the operators silently willing them to get the thing started, they kept trying for about thirty minutes, but eventually gave up. The operators were swearing down the net at them but that wouldn't get the motorbike started. North Det was in a tricky position; they had put everything on the two terrorists arriving at the service station and intercepting them there. Now that was not going to happen and there was no Plan B. Had they kept an observation post at the outhouse and a number of operators' vehicles in the vicinity, they would have been able to move in and catch the two in possession of an automatic weapon. Questions would be asked by JCU-NI HQ in Lisburn as to why the operation had been set up in the manner it had been.

The two men left the site immediately and we were stood down for that night. We remained in Omagh for another few days, hoping that another attempt would be made. A few nights later someone did return to the outhouse. Everyone was hoping that we were back on again and this time they would be able to get the bike to start. Unfortunately, a petrol bomb was tossed into the outhouse, destroying it and the motorbike. We all withdrew from Omagh back to Ballykelly, an opportunity to take two terrorists and a weapon off the streets of Northern Ireland missed. Glenn would have serious questions to answer. North Det's reputation as one of the most successful Dets was once more damaged.

The two terrorists who had been due to carry out the attack remained at large throughout my remaining time at North Det. I often wondered what happened to them. One thing is for sure, they had no idea that it was their lack of driving skills that had saved their lives that Friday night.

20 MAD DOG

From where I was sitting in the cockpit of the Gazelle, the landing pad at East Det looked not much bigger than a five-penny piece, squeezed into an impossibly tight space between their laden communications mast and the high perimeter fence. As we descended, I was certain we were going to clip something, spin out of control and plummet to the ground. I was wrong. But it did foreshadow the climax of this operation.

*

I was travelling with two North Det operators in the helicopter, while another two were travelling in their vehicles from Ballykelly to Palace Barracks, all at the request of the East Det Opso. Though he wasn't pleased, Glenn had agreed to let four operators and a technician go 'for a couple of days and no more ... whether or not the operation is completed'. He was adamant.

It was the week before Christmas, so none of us wanted to be part of a prolonged operation. I was in two minds about the whole thing. On the one hand, it would be a new experience, an insight into another Det, and one of the few operations involving Loyalist paramilitaries that I would be involved in. On the other hand, it involved one of the highest-profile Loyalists of them all: Johnny 'Mad Dog' Adair, and our brief was not the one we would have hoped for.

Johnny Adair was an Ulster Defence Association (UDA) brigadier from West Belfast and originally a hero in the Loyalist movement. He had been at the forefront of Loyalist paramilitaries since I was a teenager. He spent the 1990s in and out of prison for terrorist offences and on 15 May 2002 was once again released from Maghaberry prison in Northern Ireland, having served twenty-one months. He returned to his home in Boundary Way, West Belfast, to be met by hundreds of supporters, a fireworks display and the five other brigadiers that made up the UDA command. They were there at the request of John White, Adair's closest associate, in the hope their presence would demonstrate a show of strength and unity within the organisation. White and Adair went hand in hand and had a mutually beneficial relationship, White giving Adair some credibility and Adair providing White with the strength he needed to represent the Loyalist community.

However, none of the five other brigadiers actually wanted to be there or have anything to do with Adair. He had become obsessed with his own image, courting the media like a celebrity at every opportunity, and putting down his fellow commanders in public. He took a job as a prisoner welfare officer, trying to persuade the public that he had gone straight. It fooled nobody.

On 10 June 2002, Mark 'Swinger' Fulton was found dead in his prison cell in Maghaberry prison. He had hanged himself. Adair had been involved in drug dealing with Fulton and now planned to seize the opportunity to expand his empire. The tit-for-tat shootings between the UDA and Loyalist Volunteer Force (LVF) that resulted, thought by many to have been instigated or approved by Adair, was the final straw for the UDA command. A meeting of the UDA's inner council, including Adair, was called. The meeting was heated and came to an abrupt halt. Adair left immediately but was followed by members of the UDA straight to a meeting with the LVF in Ballysillan, where he relayed the whole story of the meeting.

On 25 September 2002, a statement from the UDA

dismissed Adair from its ranks, saying, 'As a result of ongoing investigations, the present Brigadier in West Belfast is no longer acceptable in our organisation.' Adair was furious and dismissed the statement as worthless.

East Det acquired solid intelligence that an attempt was to be made on Adair's life. The Loyalist paramilitary ranks apparently leaked like a sieve, but on this occasion the information hadn't come from an informer but from a listening device in the home of one of the UDA's top commanders. After years of pandering to him, they had finally had enough and wanted him gone for good. The hit was to be carried out by two of the UDA's most experienced hitmen. They would use one of their favourite assassination methods, a drive-by. Two men on a motorbike would approach Adair, pull up beside him, and the passenger would spray him with bullets. It was brutal but effective – the kind of thing Adair would probably have planned himself.

The intelligence was so good that East Det even knew when and where, a very rare situation. He was to be hit as he walked his eight-year-old daughter to school. That presented a problem. Word came down that the risk to the little girl and her schoolmates was unacceptable and so East Det was instructed to intervene. Had it been Adair's son Jonathan or even his wife Gina at risk, there probably would not have been an intervention: Jonathan Adair, for instance, had become an even bigger thug than his father, so much so that he had been subjected to a number of punishment beatings and shootings by Adair's own men (something Adair denied having any knowledge of). Even with the risk to an eight-year-old girl, some people were still very uncomfortable with the idea of an operation to save Adair.

East Det's compound, 500 metres from where I had first taken the Oath of Allegiance, consisted of a number of old buildings and Portakabins, nowhere near as roomy or lavish as North Det. The briefing room was tiny, and cramming us all in was difficult.

After a brief introduction, East Det's operations officer went through the various options we had of preventing the assassination, and asked for our views. The possibility of neutralising the assassins beforehand was ruled out as we didn't know where they were coming from, only when and where they would hit. A 'hard stop' – which involves a vehicle loaded with operators smashing into the target vehicle and the operators subduing the dazed occupants in whatever ways required – was also ruled out as it would give away the fact that we had prior knowledge of the attack. Our sources would be compromised. In the end, it was agreed to keep it as low-key as possible. We would put in a controlled crash and make it look like a normal everyday accident. The Opso surmised, 'They are likely to scarper once they're off the bike, but if they decide to stand and make an issue of it, we'll have plenty of back-up and the PSNI ready to respond.'

Everyone was given their role for the next morning. The North Det operators would hold back and only be used in case things went pear-shaped. I spent that night changing the encryption fills on the North Det vehicle and giving the East Det tech a hand with changing over some of his vehicles for the following morning. East Det were snowed under with operations and their poor sod of a technician was at breaking point.

Early the next morning, the operators deployed on to the ground to be in position long before the UDA assassins could be out and about. Not knowing exactly which direction they were coming from posed a problem. With limited resources, the Opso spread a wide net of operator vehicles around the school. He was using the overt-surveillance cameras located around Belfast to his full advantage, and the Gazelle was flying high above Belfast city on the lookout for the motorcycle in the traffic below. At the same time a covert camera in one of East Det's own specialist surveillance vehicles had eyes on Adair's front door waiting for him to leave. The crash vehicle was a van driven by an East Det operator, and there were two other operators in the back, ready to spring out if the UDA men decided to fight.

'Standby! Standby! Charlie One is foxtrot towards the school,' the Opso announced, having picked up Adair leaving the house via the covert camera. The operators in their surveillance cars drove by, keeping tabs on Adair's progress. There was still no sign of the motorbike at first. Everyone was on edge.

Then came the call. 'Standby! Standby! Motorcycle approaching, two-up.' The van driver picked up their route, and as the motorbike rounded the next corner he accelerated from behind and clipped the rear wheel. The bike spun out and hit the ground. The two men's instinct to get up and run kicked in and off they went. The van was driven back to base, destined for the scrapyard.

We didn't head back to North Det right away as we were invited to stay the night and celebrate a job well done, even though we hadn't contributed very much. It was the same scenario in East Det as it would have been back in Ballykelly: accompanied by copious amounts of alcohol, all the details, the what-ifs and the slip-ups of the operation were recounted, analysed and laughed at until – usually – everyone moved on to other topics of conversation. But the chatter about this operation was slower to come to an end. Everyone seemed to have opinions on Adair. All the rumours that had been circulating for years about him, about his sexuality, his drug dealing, his relationship with British Intelligence and Special Branch, were repeated. The explanation for protecting him – not wanting to risk the young girl's life – was questioned. We all knew – and it had been demonstrated on numerous occasions down the years

– that British Intelligence didn't give a damn about collateral damage from their operations if they were deemed essential.

And to many there, Adair's removal would easily have qualified as essential. Behind numerous acts of murder and violence in their area of responsibility, and many more destabilising feuds within his own organisation and community, Adair was a thorn in East Det's side. It was in most people's interests to see him gone, and yet we had just expended massive resources protecting him.

There was only one plausible explanation. Adair himself claimed he had been getting information from both British Intelligence and Special Branch on Republican targets for years, and we all knew that was a two-way street: It was suspected by all at East Det that Adair must surely have also been providing information on his own organisation to the Security Services.

If it was the case, he wouldn't have been the first double agent in Northern Ireland's history.

He was arrested again on 10 January 2003 and returned to prison. The internal feuding in the UDA continued until A and B companies withdrew their support for Adair and issued an ultimatum to C company to join them within forty-eight hours or face the consequences. They did so, almost to a man. Adair and his closest associates, including White, had to flee to Scotland. Such was the danger they were in, and rush to get away, Adair's two pet Alsatians were left behind. He was, however, joined by Gina and their children, who had to be given a police escort to the ferry at Larne.

As for us, we packed up and left East Det, a little worse for wear from the previous night. Usually the whole drinking and hangover thing helps you forget and move on from the ins and outs, the whys and wherefores of an operation. This one, though, continued to bother me and bothers me to this day. I have to keep telling myself it was the young girl's life we were saving – not Adair's.

21 LADY LUCK

Our DSM for much of my time at North Det was a six-foot-two-inch bald, cockney who – even though he spent as many weekends as he could in either Portrush or Portstewart trying to bed any woman who would have him – still believed that he could walk around Derry and the villages of South Armagh without being pinged. Truth be told, the operators in general were incredibly loose when it came to sleeping around, and it surprised me that the IRA hadn't set more 'honey traps' for them. They might have destroyed North Det's ability to operate in Northern Ireland a lot sooner.

*

'Juliet is foxtrot towards blue nine,' Sharon Op whispered into the microphone hidden in the collar of her jacket. It was very early on a Sunday morning in June and she was making her way on foot deep into the Shantallow area of Derry city, having left her surveillance car at the top of the street. The Shantallow was still lively from the Saturday night before, with plenty of revellers still about. She was following our Charlie One, a member of a Derry/Donegal-based Real IRA cell.

Sharon was a veteran operator at JCU-NI with multiple tours under her belt, but she was getting nervous, and that was not good. She had noticed a number of lingering stares that morning, more than she usually got. She got plenty of looks generally from people thanks to her blonde hair, deeply tanned skin and ample bosom, but today the looks were different. They were looks that asked, what are you doing here?

Glenn ordered a few of the other operators in the vicinity to close in and be ready to provide support if things went south.

Then, suddenly, Charlie One came to a dead stop and turned around. He looked her straight in the eye. As she was trained to do, Sharon simply smiled politely with surprise on her face and kept walking. One of the other operators moved in to take over as Charlie One continued on his way. Maybe it was Sharon's good looks that wrong-footed him and prevented him from confronting her fully and trying to find out who she was. Who knows!

Thinking all she had to do now was make her way back to her surveillance vehicle and get back to base, Sharon relaxed. But she was in for another shock when she saw thick black smoke rising up ahead, from exactly where she had parked. She called 'Standby! Standby!' and the radio net fell silent, awaiting word from her. As she crested the hill, she saw that her car was going up in flames, having clearly been petrol-bombed. She sent a series of clicks on her covert body communications kit, letting the operations room and the other operators know that she was unable to speak.

Glenn immediately panned one of the overt-surveillance cameras to the car, giving him a full view of Sharon as she approached the burning vehicle. It was surrounded by a gang of youths cheering at the sight. Being the pro she was, there was no way she could break her stride suddenly and attract attention, so she simply gripped her SIG sauer 9mm pistol within her bag, ready to draw and fire if needs be, and kept walking.

The other operators were within striking distance, poised to pounce if the crowd so much as twitched in her direction. It was amazing to hear the calmness in her voice as she got past the scene without being confronted: 'Juliet is clear.

Requesting pick-up.' Glenn responded in the same, almost bored, tone: 'Roger, Juliet. Take your next left. November will extract you.'

Sharon was brought in safely, but the situation was not yet under control. The surveillance vehicle still had to be retrieved: we needed to know if it had been broken into or if any of the surveillance kit or weapons had been taken. If they had, there would be serious repercussions. Soon the fire service and the PSNI had arrived in numbers, and the flames were dowsed and the crowd dispersed. Glenn made a call to the spanners bay: 'Retrieve that vehicle, now!'

The Spanners had their own recovery truck – bearing the name of a fictitious company – in which they would head into Derry to get Sharon's vehicle. Jim Spanner had left the Det by now; Mac and Al were in charge. Mac Spanner wasn't exactly thrilled about the idea of going into the Shantallow, given the circumstances, but he had no choice. Anyhow, the vehicle was now being secured by the PSNI and he would be escorted in by two other PSNI Landrovers: more than enough to keep him safe. It wasn't long before a relieved Mac arrived and lowered the car into the tech bay. A crowd, including Sharon, Glenn and myself, gathered to see the damage. Luck was on our side: there was no sign of any theft but the weapons and kit were a write-off.

With her cover blown so completely, Sharon's time at North Det was, by necessity, over; but her time at JCU-NI was not. Reflecting how much respect the top brass at JCU-NI had for her and how much they valued her experience, she was transferred to Aldergrove where she would work at 7 SCT, rather than back to her parent unit as would normally be the case.

By now I should have been safely back at JCU-NI HQ in Lisburn, myself; redeployed, as planned, to Cameras for my final months. However, I had been asked to stay for this one last operation. Dave Tech, who was taking over from me at

North Det, had only arrived a week earlier. Glenn didn't want to drop him straight into a live operation and so here I was, still on the job.

The briefing for this one was a bit sketchy, the intelligence wasn't 100 per cent reliable (in other words, it had come from some informer), and the details on the target were scarce. The gist was that an attack of some sort was to be launched against the PSNI in Derry in the coming days by a Derry/Donegal-based Real IRA cell. It was thought to be a mortar, which it was believed would come from a weapons cache located somewhere in the Shantallow area of the city. Not exactly confidence-building, but Glenn would have to work with it just the same. We had a single name to begin with, a young man in his early twenties from Derry and a known Real IRA sympathiser. He would take Charlie One status for now, until a bigger fish came along.

From surveillance on Charlie One, it was quickly established where the weapons hide was located in the Shantallow. Glenn planned a covert insertion into the house to place a tracking device on the mortar, allowing the operators to keep their distance from the target and avoid spooking anyone.

This wasn't how an insertion would normally be done. The usual weeks of surveillance had to be skipped, given the tight time frame. The fact that the house appeared to be empty, other than when Charlie One visited, was seen to be enough to make it worth the risk. The location was favourable for the insertion, in that the house backed on to a green area that could be used to approach the house unseen. Once more our friend 'Bill' from 'Box' was drafted in.

It was 0100 hours and quiet as a morgue when the three men pulled up at the green area behind the house. The car was parked up within line of sight of one of Glenn's cameras. The other operators kept their distance, but minutes away should they be needed.

The insertion team used the cover of the tree line, in full summer bloom, to make their way to the rear garden. The garden gate was unlocked and they got to the rear door. There had been no time to do a full survey with the result that no key had been cut in the CMOE cell for this job, so the lock was picked. The door was opened and to everyone's relief no unidentified alarm sounded that would require Bill's urgent expertise. Instead he went about searching for any hidden alarm systems or CCTV cameras, while the two operators searched the house for the weapons cache. It took longer than they would have liked but the cache was eventually located in an attack space covered by a huge tarpaulin. The operators worked quickly and silently, making sure that the neighbours didn't hear them working as they inserted the tracking device into the mortar. It would take an expert to find it, such was its minute size. Job done, the men made their way from the house, careful to leave it exactly as they had found it.

Once back at North Det, their photographs were developed and revealed an array of timers, detonators, ammunition and, of course, the mortar and firing tube: a great result. Now it was just a case of locating the others in the group and waiting for the tracking device to show that the mortar was on the move.

Charlie One was making regular trips over the border towards Donegal, but his meetings with Derry Real IRA members were few. This led to speculation that he would provide the mortar while those from Donegal would carry out the actual attack.

Early on Sunday, 15 June, Charlie One visited the weapons cache again, stayed for approximately thirty minutes and left, heading across the border once more, though not before making a call.

In an admirable effort at counter-surveillance, he had been using a public payphone in the Shantallow area.

Though the paramilitaries had caught on to the problems of using mobile phones, they were still under the impression that random public telephones were safe to use. The truth was JCU-NI simply had to dial in a code to Government Communication HQ in Cheltenham, and all calls from any phone would be recorded. To make things even easier, once the target had made their call from a monitored phone, if an operator went straight to the phone after them, the call could be instantly replayed to us in the operations room.

So, when Charlie One made his unsuspecting call from the now monitored payphone that Sunday morning, and Jack Op was in like a shot to dial the required code, we reckoned we had him.

Unfortunately, the contents of the call suggested otherwise. North Det had been completely wrong-footed. The call from Charlie One was actually made to confirm that the 'scout vehicles' could leave from across the border. That could only mean one thing: a car bomb! (Scout vehicles were driven ahead of other vehicles to make sure the coast was clear.) Charlie One must have visited the cache that morning just to get a timer and/or detonator for the now imminent car bomb attack. The intelligence that North Det had been provided with was totally wrong.

Touts! Glenn must have cursed. He immediately started deploying any spare operators to cover the border crossings, hoping against hope to pick up a sign of a scout vehicle or the bomb vehicle itself. RCG warned PSNI patrols to be on the lookout, too. All of North Det's camera resources, both overt and covert, were dedicated to finding the approaching vehicle-borne IED. The remainder of the operators were kept on Charlie One in the hope that he would lead us to the device. We were clutching at straws, facing the prospect of a car bomb of unknown size going off in some unknown location in Northern Ireland. Again.

As luck would have it, that's when Sharon was spotted by

lookouts, known as 'dickers', around the Shantallow area, and had her cover blown. It was a serious blow for our already stretched resources trailing Charlie One but, ironically, it spooked Charlie One enough to make him act. From intelligence gathered later by North Det, it turned out that he had immediately contacted one of the scout vehicles and warned them that we could be on to them.

Fortunately for us, a red Toyota Hiace van was then spotted acting suspiciously by a PSNI patrol, which followed the vehicle as it made its way along the Clooney Road. By the time the van was reached, it had been abandoned and those driving it had made their escape, probably in one of the scout vehicles.

The bomb inside was defused by army bomb disposal teams. It contained 1200lb of explosives, twice the size of the Omagh bomb. It would have caused untold devastation had it exploded anywhere in the city.

North Det had been lucky beyond belief. And nobody but us knew it.

It was the last major operation that I would be involved with at North Det and though I would visit there many times again over the coming twelve months and return for my leaving party, it would never be the same. It would be a few months yet before I could slip away from North Det to start the next part of my JCU-NI adventure.

22 THE ARSE

'We don't want a crowd to build up before we even get you techs in there, or worse for a shooter to have time to set up and open fire on you.'

*

JCU-NU HQ at Lisburn was known as 'The Arse' for a reason, and not a good one. Life there was completely different to life at one of the Dets. It had structure, which wasn't in and of itself a bad thing, but it also had internal politics to go with that structure, which was.

Unlike at North Det where, as a technician, you were permanently on call, at Cameras section in the Arse two technicians took the duty pagers for a week at a time. It gave you the luxury of knowing that when you knocked off work at the end of a day you were finished, and it made planning leave much easier. I had a considerable number of leave days accumulated from my time at North Det, and I planned to use them all.

In command at Cameras was Ted, a huge Scottish staff sergeant and one of the best bosses I ever worked for. Ted understood that my last two years at North Det had been a nightmare and so, while he made the most of the experience I had gained during that time for his own department, he also cut me a lot of slack.

I knew most of the other guys at Cameras already, although there were some unfamiliar faces that had only recently arrived at JCU-NI. I got a few of the usual odd ('a

Paddy?') looks initially, but those didn't last long.

The worst part about being here was the backbiting: the seemingly endless efforts by some to climb up through the ranks, often at the expense of others. There had been no place for that at North Det, in fact any sign of it would have seen you sent packing. I had little interest in promotions, even though I had been fortunate enough to get them; I enjoyed being a technician too much.

Nonetheless, I had some very interesting times at Cameras. It more than played its part in the murky world of British Intelligence in Northern Ireland. It was truly amazing to look at the map board in the workshop and see the number of surveillance cameras that JCU-NI had under its control all over Northern Ireland, from the dozens dotted around Belfast and Derry city to the isolated hilltop masts down in Tyrone, Armagh and Down.

Since my training at Cameras over two years previously, new camera systems had been added whose capabilities were far greater, whose range had doubled to almost 4km, and which had built-in infrared and thermal-imaging systems. They were, however, still big and bulky, and that meant installing them was hard work.

Just like at North Det, all rigging work was done at night but all the preparations were done during the day at the workshops. Not long into my first week I arrived early at the workshops, as was my habit, and let myself in. As I was getting set up, I noticed a camera controller and monitor in the corner of the test bay, which I assumed was used to test the cameras before they were deployed on the ground, so over I went to have a closer look.

I logged into the controller using my North Det log-in code but to my complete surprise, in fact shock, it wasn't the signal from the camera in the test bay that came up on the screen, but from the camera located at Masonic mast in Derry city. North Det's camera on display here? What was going on, I wondered.

I went through the list of North Det cameras that I had committed to memory, typing in the address of each one, and every time that camera's view popped up on the screen in front of me. I went over to the office and retrieved the list of all the JCU-NI camera addresses in Northern Ireland, again typing in any of them I was able to bring them up to view.

Holy shit!

My first thought was that the operations officers in each of the Dets would have a fit if they knew that Cameras section at HQ could control their cameras, but more importantly that they had eyes on everything that the Det had under surveillance. For security and turf reasons, the Dets guarded their information like lionesses watching over their cubs, and shared it with nobody, not even the other Dets, unless they really had to.

I logged out of the system and waited for Ted to arrive. I now had a real dilemma on my hands. I had spent over two years at North Det and my loyalty, even if it was sometimes tested, was unwavering at that time. Shouldn't I tell Glenn in Ballykelly? Now, though, I was part of a new team. So shouldn't I just keep quiet?

The other technicians began to arrive and as soon as I saw Ted make his way to his office, I walked over and knocked on the door.

'Any chance of a quiet word, Ted?' Ted was an extremely easy-going bloke … until you crossed him!

'No worries, Seán. Close the door. What's up?' He was always cheery in the morning, no matter what was on the table.

'I logged into the controller in the test bay this morning …' I didn't need to add anything further; Ted knew exactly what I had discovered.

'Seán, we need to have access to those cameras. Half the

faults we're called out to are due to operator error. You know that yourself. I don't have the manpower to deploy a team to every site for every supposed fault. We can log in here and bring the cameras back online remotely. It's so much more most efficient that way.' He was right, of course, but that still didn't excuse the breach in security: none of the guys here were cleared to view what was on many of those cameras. Neither was I, in truth.

'All hell would break loose if the operations officers find out, Ted.'

He grinned back at me. 'They'll only find out if someone tells them, Seán. I could order you to keep quiet but I won't. I'll leave it up to you. I know this puts you in an awkward position.'

I left the room and went about my tasks for the day, pondering my situation. It was typical of the trouble with JCU-NI: there were always secrets within secrets.

Later that week, dressed in green army uniform, we piled into the back of two armoured army Landrovers, two teams of two technicians. There was a lead vehicle in front and a rear vehicle to give further protection. We were part of what was known at Cameras as a 'green move'. Pretty soon, we were all sweating profusely, not because it was warm that night, but because we were in there with four other soldiers and all our equipment, and feeling anxious.

We had arrived at Girdwood Barracks on the Crumlin Road in Belfast from Lisburn earlier that night in our civilian vehicles, but our final destination was far too dangerous for anything but a green army patrol. The briefing from the patrol commander, a young lieutenant who looked barely old enough to shave, left us in no doubt.

'We will leave here at 0100 hours. The technicians will ride in the middle two vehicles, the other two providing cover front and rear. We will take a roundabout route. Once on-site things must move quickly, we can't hang about. We'll pull right up on to the pavement and the doors will open. My guys out first and secure the area. Next, technicians. The COP on-site will have come down in the lift and secured the ground floor of the building. They will hold the lift until you get in with your kit. You'll then be taken to the roof. I can't stress enough how quickly you need to move, and I'm sorry but I can't give you any men to help with your equipment. Any questions? No? Good!'

The infamous Divis flats complex had been constructed in the 1960s as a solution to the growing slum problem that plagued Belfast city at the time. The Divis Tower, standing at over 200 feet and twenty stories high, dominated the skyline. Located near the flashpoint of the interface of the Falls and Shankill roads, it ended up playing a strategic role for the British army for over forty years. Due to intense IRA activity in the area during the 1970s, including snipers firing at British army patrols, the top two floors of the Divis Tower were taken over by the British army. Despite the obvious problems with inserting troops and supplies, with access often only available via helicopter, the arrangement remained in place.

Now the tower provided East Det with an invaluable vantage point for its overt, high-powered surveillance cameras. Maintaining them was, however, a nightmare for Cameras section.

As we drove to the flats, I reflected on my decision about HQ's monitoring of all these overt camera feeds. I had decided to say nothing in the end, as I didn't think it was my place to do so. I was taken from my thoughts by a shout from the front cab of the Landrover.

'Standby! Two minutes to debus.' The soldiers in the rear of the vehicle cocked their weapons, standard British army SA80 assault rifles, and checked the safety catches. We were only armed with our SIG sauer 9mm pistols, there being no room for our HK53 assault rifles.

The Landrover mounted the pavement with a jolt and came to a loud halt. The doors flew open and the four soldiers fanned out, weapons aimed outwards. At the same time, I could see the soldiers from the COP holding the entrance door for us. We jumped from the vehicle and grabbed our kit, which weighed well over 100kg. We struggled to move it at speed and to get into the lifts. While the Landrovers departed to wait back at base for us, the COP soldiers squeezed in and we trundled all the way to the top floor.

The top two floors of the Divis Tower were overflowing with surveillance equipment of all sorts, from high-powered binoculars to high-resolution cameras, but nothing compared to the two JCU-NI cameras mounted on the corners of the rooftop. I could see why East Det valued them so much, but there was no time to admire. We were there to replace a faulty camera on which the night-vision mode was no longer working. It was now close to 0200 hours and knowing that the team from Girdwood Barracks would not risk a daylight extraction, we knew we had to get a move on or wait until the following night.

Fortunately, we were all experienced technicians and riggers and had the job done in good time. Slightly exhausted by the time the COP commander sent the message to Girdwood that we were ready for extraction, we waited.

We hadn't been briefed on the extraction method but reasonably assumed that it would be the reverse of the insertion. Which it was, with one difference.

Insertion times into Divis Tower are always varied so as to prevent a pattern being established. Once you are in, those in the area know that you have to come out, and are usually waiting. It was Paul who spotted the small crowd that had gathered on the corner below – not large or menacing but, as we knew, still with the potential to turn very quickly.

The COP commander waited for the radio call to let him know the extraction team was approaching, then we were bundled into the lifts with our kit. The COP soldiers sprinted from the lift and took up their positions; this time, I noticed, not quite as far outside as they were earlier. Something told me that they knew something we didn't.

We made for the doors, slowed by our equipment, arms and legs screaming from the effort but adrenaline driving us on. As we exited the building we could see the doors of the Landrovers being held open for us. The two men holding the doors were yelling, 'Get a fucking move on!' The crowd that had gathered was by now throwing rocks, bottles and chunks of pavement at us. Any fatigue I had felt disappeared and I found myself sprinting. The COP soldiers withdrew as we reached the Landrovers, and the first petrol bomb landed as we were dragged unceremoniously into the vehicles, which had already started moving off before the doors were banged shut.

To say we were shaken was an understatement, but everyone in our Landrover was pissing themselves laughing. 'Welcome to the Divis flats!' one of the young privates yelled over the engine.

It wasn't all hard work and no play at HQ. Apart from the wild parties, plenty of other opportunities came our way from time to time. One was a six-man expedition to Corsica put together by the new workshops staff sergeant, Ski, who just happened to be a mate of mine. I jumped at the chance: three weeks' hill-walking across the GR20 mountain range in glorious sunshine at the expense of the British army. Nothing could have been better. Ski put a great team together, all good guys who were both capable climbers and good company. It made for a brilliant three weeks: the views were stunning from some of the best hills I have ever climbed; the people were amazing; and we even got to spend time with some of the French Foreign Legion soldiers stationed there, which was fascinating.

By the time I got back to JCU-NI I had only a few months left, and while I carried out many more installation and repair jobs everywhere from Belfast to Derry and further afield, it was the withdrawal of British troops and the downgrading of the Dets and their surveillance assets that would dominate my final months.

23 WITHDRAWAL METHODS

The British army air corps Lynx helicopter was spacious enough for the three technicians, myself included, who were travelling from Lisburn that evening. JCU-NI's own Gazelle helicopters wouldn't have the space for the equipment we were going in to extract, and so a call had been put in to the army air corps. We were heading to a hilltop site near to Belleek in Co. Fermanagh, close to the border with Donegal. The site was inaccessible by road and even if it had been accessible, it wasn't safe for military to travel by car to such an exposed site this close to the border. During the bad old days, only a few years previously, when the Provisional IRA had still been very active, sniper and mortar attacks had been frequent in the area, and while the dissident Republican movement had yet to get to that operational level, the risks remained.

The helicopter flared as we reached the isolated site and we moved quickly towards the communications hut, making sure not to be blown over by the downdraft from the blades. The helicopter was only on the ground for a few seconds before taking off again to safety, due back early in the morning for us, by which time we would be laden down with a full surveillance-camera installation.

The isolated nature of this site meant that we were quite a bit away from any support should we get into any bother, so we all had our standard-issue pistols and assault rifles with extra magazines, just in case. The communications hut itself was of sturdy construction, so my plan, if anything kicked off, was to close the steel door and await the cavalry.

The surveillance camera was mounted on top of a 100-foot mast and, given its already elevated position on the top of a hill, it offered unbeatable views of Fermanagh and Donegal. Not much could move on either side of the border without this surveillance camera picking it up. The camera was under the control of South Det and I couldn't imagine the operations officer there being happy to lose such an asset.

We couldn't climb the mast until nightfall, of course, so we set about stripping out the control equipment, power supplies and cables in the communications hut first. Not so much as a cable tie could be left behind to show that JCU-NI had ever been there. While two of us worked, the other kept watch on the approaches to the site. We worked like that in shifts until darkness fell.

Under cover of darkness, I climbed the mast and attached a harness to the 40kg camera while the other two lads remained below to lower it to the ground. The weather closed in on us, with thick mist rolling in fast over the hills, but being hardy technicians we worked on regardless and by midnight we were done and had put in the call over the radio net to request extraction. Unfortunately, it seemed not everyone was so hardy and we were told we would have to hold out until the weather cleared before the helicopter would make the journey. If it didn't clear by first light, we would have to wait until the next evening.

We resigned ourselves to waiting until the next evening and prepared accordingly. We took it in turns to be on watch through the night, and before first light the Lynx was back for us, the rhythm of its rotor blades clearly audible in the still morning air. We loaded up over 150kg of equipment and took off for Lisburn.

This uneventful, drama-free, relatively straightforward mission was actually the beginning of the end for JCU-NI ... or so I thought.

*

The hilltop site near Belleek was one of the last British military installations left along the border. The ongoing peace process was bringing about a reduction in British troop numbers and the closure of bases throughout Northern Ireland.

JCU-NI wasn't exempt, either: many of its most important sites were to close. It began with Ebrington Barracks on the Clooney Road in Derry, a place I knew well. Ted from Cameras called us to a briefing by first thing one morning.

'Orders from upstairs: effective today, we are to start the process of stripping out sites. I'll be splitting you into teams so we can work around the clock and get it done quickly. Terry and Seán, head for Ebrington this morning and do a survey on what needs doing and how long it will take.' He added an aside: 'Swing by North Det first, Seán; Glenn Opso wants a quick word with you before you head into the city.'

I knew what that would be about: Glenn would rightly be fuming at the loss of the cameras from Ebrington. He had two there that gave him not only a view over the Waterside but right into the heart of Derry city. What Glenn thought I could do about it was beyond me, but I'd pop in anyway.

Terry and I got our gear together and headed for North Det. I headed straight for the operations room once we arrived, while Terry went for a chat with the techs. At the time, I was still welcome to come and go as I pleased at North Det, though that would change soon, I realised. I was no longer a North Det tech and my privileges would soon be removed: I was no longer part of the team.

'Seán! Good to see you. How's things at the Arse? I believe you're heading into Ebrington to start the strip-out.' He seemed pretty relaxed about it.

'Look, Glenn,' I said, trying to pre-empt him, 'there is absolutely nothing I can do about those cameras; and let me tell you, there's worse to come. Clooney, Masonic and Rosemount are all on the list, too, and that's just for starters, I would think. They'll eventually start stripping the civilian and police sites as well, I'm sure. It's a disaster.'

We both knew that losing those sites would remove North Det's ability to see into the Bogside, Shantallow and the Creggan, and thereby weaken its effectiveness against the dissidents. But to my surprise, Glenn didn't seem in the least bit perturbed by this; in fact, he had this grin that said he was in the know about something that I wasn't:

'No worries. We'll manage, Seán. Just wondering if you could do me a quick favour while you're in the city? There is a little PSNI compound just down the road from Ebrington; it's pretty new and I want a quick site survey done. On the quiet, that is. I need to know what kind of a view I can get from an overt and maybe even a covert from the mast in there. Could you take a quick look for me?' This didn't make any sense: Mark Tech was more than capable of doing this, and I said so to Glenn, but he just replied: 'Well, you're going to be part of something else pretty soon and I think it's best if you do it.'

I knew better than to argue any further, so I grabbed some breakfast, caught up with a few of the lads I knew at the Det, and headed for the city. Stripping out Ebrington and Clooney would be hard work as there was a lot of equipment and cable to be taken down off the mast. Time for a trade-off with Glenn, I figured. I got on the radio to him and said I'd only have time to do his site survey if he let the technicians from Cameras sleep at North Det. It would save the hours of driving time to and from Lisburn each night. Although it wasn't the done thing, he agreed.

I eventually headed for Glenn 's 'little PSNI compound' not far from the Waterside Hospital. I found a relatively new installation, the mast in the middle of the compound almost bare and a brand-new communications hut at the base, identical to those used by JCU-NI at other sites. Why was a new site being established, I wondered, when the rest of the network seemed to be in its final days? Something fishy was going on, I realised, but as yet I was in the dark.

Even though it was still daylight, I knew I wouldn't be up there for long and so without even hooking up a harness I quickly scaled the mast. The view across the water was excellent and would serve well for both an overt and covert camera installation. I made my way down just as quickly and began to think things over as we headed back to Lisburn to brief Ted. That mast had been put there with surveillance cameras in mind, without a doubt. With the likely closure of bases, including North Det's home at Shackleton, I thought what was the point? And what was this 'something else' I was going to be part of that Glenn mentioned? I had very little time left at JCU-NI and wasn't looking to do much but wind down.

A few days later I received a call from Gary Opso at HQ to attend a meeting at Aldergrove that afternoon and to bring Terry with me. It didn't sound like a question, really, so I went. I asked Ted if he knew what it was about but he had no idea. It didn't matter to him in terms of workload, though, since Cameras and Radios were doing more stripping out work now than they were doing repairs and installations.

We arrived at Aldergrove that afternoon and made our way down to the end of the disused runway where the JCU-NI had its secure compound. We found Gary in the cookhouse, waiting with four other technicians, two from Aldergrove Det, and two from Radios at Lisburn. We followed them through the vast hangars that acted as the home for the Aldergrove Dets and up to the high barrier that separated the compound from a construction site. There had been major work going for the last few months on the new accommodation building for Det staff, which we all knew about. Gary lifted one of the barriers and we all went through.

As well as accommodation blocks, though, it turns out there was also a brand-new state-of-the-art operations room being constructed in secret. Plasma screens for the monitor wall; touch-screen controllers for the surveillance cameras mounted on the operations officer's desk; purpose-built work stations for the spooks and bleeps behind the desk like nothing I had ever seen before; and three helicopter landing pads were planned, along with enough hangar space to hold the tech and spanner bays and store the surveillance vehicles for two Dets. We were also shown the next generation of surveillance vehicles. The communications system in them was like nothing we had seen before and the covert cameras that were fitted were far beyond anything we ever had. Even as an experienced surveillance technician, I would have had difficulty spotting the equipment.

JCU-NI wasn't winding down at all! They were simply relocating and regrouping ahead of the closure of their outposts. There were two of these operations buildings planned in this new compound – more than enough room for North and East Det to move to, if and when their own bases shut down. Aldergrove would be the last British army base to close, ensuring that JCU-NI could operate for a long time to come.

No wonder the operations officers at the Dets hadn't been as bothered as I expected them to be at the loss of some of their camera sites – they knew that they were getting a more advanced surveillance system in their place.

I still didn't know what all this had to do with me, considering I was leaving within a few months. Gary enlightened me.

'Even though everything is being fed back to Aldergrove, we still have to be able to operate all over Northern Ireland; hence the new surveillance vehicles. We're going to trial them in a few areas over the next few weeks and see how they work. I'll be acting as the Opso back at Aldergrove, while you rig the transmitter receivers on different sites around Derry and Belfast. A kind of test run, if you like; we'll check how well the communications and cameras work from the surveillance vehicles and test patching the overt cameras back there, too. We also have a couple of new overt-surveillance cameras that we want to test. When it's all over, we'll compile a report between us.'

The surveillance assets located at police stations and civilian sites around Northern Ireland weren't going to be part of the extraction, either.

'One final thing: this doesn't go any further than us. Very few people know about this yet. Let's keep it that way.'

Over the next few months we installed the new system in various locations and it worked perfectly. It was almost flawless in its clarity and consistency. Even in areas that we would normally have experienced dead spots for communications and imagery, it came up trumps. Gary was thrilled.

Ebrington and Clooney Barracks were closed in 2003 and the troops moved to Shackleton Barracks in Ballykelly. The other outposts, Masonic and Rosemount in Derry, followed suit. The closure of Shackleton itself – which would see North Det leave its home of forty years – didn't happen until March 2008.

I had misjudged JCU-NI, thinking they were withdrawing too soon and underestimating the dissident movement. But JCU-NI was simply shifting with the changing political landscape, subtly as ever. The future of surveillance looked bright and secure in Northern Ireland and further afield.

The report that was compiled by the end of the trials on the new system was extremely positive. So much so, it was soon adopted in the battle against a new terrorist threat in the UK: that from Islamic extremists. Many of my friends from North Det would go on to work in that arena using the skills they had acquired on the streets of Northern Ireland.

24 NÍ BHEIDH ÁR LEITHÉIDÍ ARÍS ANN

He was referring to a night the previous Christmas when a few of us went on a bit of a bender in Portstewart. We got a taxi back to Ballykelly and made our way to the main entrance of the barracks. The walk from there to the compound was about a mile and a half and it was freezing, too cold even for snow. One of us had the great idea that we should remove an item of clothing every 100 metres. Within 500 metres of the compound we were all stark naked. By the time we made it inside, we were blue with cold and covered in mud from the so-called shortcut we'd taken across the airfield. Nonetheless, we went straight to the Det bar where we remained naked and drinking until first light. Word of our antics spread around, of course, and we got a bit of slagging, but that was it, we hoped.

*

It was October 2004 and the Royal Corps of Signals, my parent unit, wanted me back. A normal tour of duty at JCU-NI was only two years and I had already done three. But when I thought about it, I knew I could never go back to a normal green army unit where rank, shiny boots and haircuts would be the norm.

I decided to leave the British army. My partner and I decided to move back to her home country of South Africa. I was hoping that the change would ease the problems I was having.

Careerwise, my three years had been very successful in

one sense. I had been graded 'outstanding' and recommended for promotion each year in my confidential reports. I didn't get an actual promotion until the last year, but it was nice to be nominated just the same. I was actually graded the unit's top corporal three years in a row.

But all this success came at a price. It started with problems sleeping, something that was a bonus at first as the amount of work to be done was so enormous. I put it down to my workload initially, but that proved incorrect. I then began using alcohol as a way of knocking myself out, when sleep just wouldn't come. The truth was, though, it was the fear of the nightmares I was having that kept me from sleep, and alcohol was not helping.

Despite my happy-go-lucky exterior, it turned out that I was actually suffering from bouts of depression. This was before the days when post-traumatic stress disorder was acknowledged and the British army started to be proactive with regard to the mental health of its soldiers. The macho male environment of military life made it difficult to admit to such perceived weaknesses. So, despite the inner demons I was battling, I felt I had to maintain an outer mask and keep my issues to myself. Later, that strategy proved to have been a serious error on my part.

My final months were spent near Bath in the UK, where I went through the resettlement training in preparation for a return to civilian life. I reflected on my three years at JCU-NI. I was no longer the naïve soldier who had arrived at Belfast City Airport not really knowing what he had got himself in for. I had grown both as a soldier and as a person. From those early days of shock upon realising the scope of British Intelligence's surveillance capabilities, through to my drive to succeed at training and when thrown straight in at the deep end at North Det, to my final twelve months at Cameras – there had been many ups and downs; many days and weeks of routine and anticipation leading to those great moments of utter exhilaration; I had seen good men lose their careers and I had celebrated many a successful operation. In the end, I wouldn't have changed very much at all. I felt privileged to have been given a unique opportunity to view the complex situation in Northern Ireland first hand and from both sides, but I still couldn't make any sense of it. All I knew for sure was that it would never be solved using guns: they just create their own vicious circles of violence and counter-violence, surveillance and counter-surveillance.

Before I left Northern Ireland, I needed to say goodbye properly, and that involved two things: drinking and a leaving gift to be presented by me to the Det. Gifts, actually, as both North Det and Cameras were throwing parties for me.

I needed inspiration for the gifts, so I strolled along the corridors of the secure compound at North Det to take a closer look at what others before me had left behind. Everyone clearly put a lot of thought into their choice of gifts. I realised, looking at them, that long after I had left, whatever I left would be the only thing that people would have to know me by. Some were more inspiring than others, but each told its own story of life at the Det since its early days as FRU.

There was everything from paintings of famous army scenes, like *Cockleshell Heroes* (left by one of the SBS troopers), to a large, brass, wine-bottle opener mounted in the Det bar. That had been Sharon Op's leaving gift and was put to good use on a nightly basis. There was a very poignant gift hanging outside the operations room. It was a painting of the Swordfish bomber that had once flown out of Ballykelly airfield during World War II. The inscription simply read, 'To all the friends I found at North and to Hetty, the one I lost'. It was a stark reminder of how dangerous a tour at JCU-NI could be.

My favourite was left by Jim Spanner, a boogie board mounted on the wall of the bar. Inscribed in a column down its length was:

My Tour:

28 Cars
16 operators
3 OPSOs
2 OCs
3 DSMs
3 Spooks
3 Spanners
2 Chefs
2 Inkies
2 DQs
2 GDs
1 Brownie
0 Regrets

It summed up his time at North Det perfectly, and with humour. I wanted the same effect. But I was stumped, and with only a few days to go to the party, the pressure was on.

First up was the Cameras party at HQ in Lisburn. It was a Friday – the usual day for leaving drinks, and, as usual, we started in the workshop bar. A good crowd gathered, everyone glad to let off some steam on a Friday. My leaving speech was given by Terry, a young Scottish guy with whom I had worked closely during my time there. It was the usual roasting. He stood at the top of the room and called the increasingly merry crowd to order. Clearing his throat, he began in his soft Highland accent:

'Sir [addressing the CO], ladies and gentlemen, it's time to say farewell to Seán. As most of you know, Seán has been one of the longest-serving techs at JCU-NI. Firstly, at North

Det, then East Det and finally here with us at Cameras. I tried to get some dirt on him from the Dets but as usual they were keeping tight-lipped. No surprise there! Lucky I have a few of my own stories to tell.'

I started to shift uncomfortably recalling some of the many screw-ups I had made during my time.

'The first job I went on with Seán, I had only just met the guy. We were heading to Derry to do an installation and Seán was behind the wheel. I noticed that he didn't take the turn at Randalstown to follow the designated safe route through Portglenone, Limavady, Ballykelly and into Derry. Instead, he took us through the "red zone" of the Glenshane Pass and Dungiven. It was past midnight and to be honest I was thinking, "Oh fuck, this guy is handing me over to the IRA and he's going to do a runner for the border" But no, Seán was just doing what North Det does best, breaking the rules. When I asked him if it was safe going through the area, he replied "I am, but you might be fucked." It was then that I realised that Seán had a very dark sense of humour.'

There were a few one-liner jibes at me from around the room and I was hoping that was it. Unfortunately, though, it was not.

'Another job I was on with Seán was down to a PSNI station in Newtownhamilton. Seán insisted on driving again, as he knew the roads well from his time at North Det. By now, I had learned that Seán always liked to drive. We pulled up to the gates of the station and he pushed the intercom button. Letting Seán do the talking to the PSNI in South Armagh wasn't a great idea. He spoke in his thick Cork accent into the intercom, telling them we were from Lisburn. For some reason, the gate was taking forever to open and I for one was getting a bit nervous sitting outside a PSNI station in bandit country for so long. Eventually the gate was opened and we pulled in. We were met by the entire station fanning out around us, assault rifles and pistols at the ready. Seán casually lowered the window and showed his ID. The PSNI officer exploded with language a little too colourful for this gathering. Let's just say he was less than pleased.'

That got a few shouts of 'Dirty Fenian' from around the room, but all in jest.

When my turn came I kept it short and sweet. I thanked everyone for coming and said that I had thoroughly enjoyed my time at Cameras, which indeed I had. I presented Ted with my parting gift – a framed and signed Cork GAA jersey. There wouldn't be too many of those hanging on the walls of JCU-NI HQ.

Speeches over, the night properly took off and we moved from bar to bar along the strip within Thiepval Barracks at Lisburn. I slipped away without ceremony at about 1 a.m., aware that I had an early start that morning.

I drove my own personal vehicle to North Det later that day, escorted by a lead vehicle with two armed technicians from Radios. They were on their way to a job in Derry and agreed to see me as far as Ballykelly. I had never previously given it much thought, but for the first time since I'd arrived, I felt very vulnerable moving around Northern Ireland unarmed and with no armoured doors or seats on the car.

I made my way down the long road from Shackleton Barracks main gate to North Det compound for the last time. I typed in the entry code into the keypad and waited for the roller shutter gate to raise, thinking how the code would be changed again soon and I would no longer have free access to this highly classified area. That was the way of things, I thought: once you were gone, you were gone! No popping in for a coffee and a chat with the lads; you were, by necessity, ejected from their world.

I parked beside the tech bay and got ready for what would be another long day and night of farewells. North Det, like all tight-knit communities, had its traditions. All leaving parties were themed. Everyone would have to come to the party as something beginning with a particular letter of the alphabet. Tonight was 'H' night. Everything from helicopters to hangmen, harlots to hamsters and even one Hannibal Lecter showed up. I dressed as a hitman.

After a lunchtime barbecue put on by the chefs, the serious drinking began. I was being clever and pacing myself, leaving half full bottles of beer littered around the bar. Eventually, it was time for the formalities. First on the list was the yard of ale, containing approximately 2.5 pints of a drink of your own choosing. I chose bottled Guinness, hoping that the lack of gas and bubbles would make it easier to get down, but knowing that the lads would have spiked it with every spirit in the bar anyhow. The hymn, 'Jerusalem', would normally be played while you were downing the yard but, being an avid rugby fan, I wasn't too pleased at the prospect of listening to an English rugby anthem. I spotted Baz Op out of the corner of my eye by the music system with a big grin on him. As I raised the long glass to my mouth, 'The Fields of Athenry' came belting out.

It was Baz who stood up to make the farewell speech. I was glad of that: we had known it each other since he had arrived at North almost two years ago. An excellent operator, technically astute and no better man to have at your back. He would make a great Opso and I hoped he would be given the opportunity some day.

'Okay, let's all be honest! When each of us first met Seán, we weren't sure whether to shake his hand or shoot him!' That got a lot of laughs … because it was so true. 'But he settled in eventually, in fact he really settled in. As an example of how well he settled in, it would be hard to beat the story of his night out in Portstewart last Christmas. But rather than me standing here telling you the whole sordid story, why don't I let you see it for yourselves?'

Next thing, the CCTV footage, which Baz had obviously

collected on the night, with great foresight, of our naked escapades, was being projected on a screen on the rear wall of the bar. Thank God I was so drunk by that stage that the embarrassment passed over me.

Video finished and the laughter now dying out, I stood to say my own few words. Again, I kept it simple, and finished with something slightly sentimental but also playing up my reputation.

'Friendships were never encouraged at JCU-NI, but despite that I have made many. To those who I count among my friends here, I thank you for an amazing three years. To those I don't and who have managed to piss me off, be careful: you never know when I might decide to go over to the other side.' Amongst all those laughing were a few newer faces who looked a little worried.

Glenn presented me with an Orange Order sash. It had been rescued by the Det from a fire in an Orange hall that had been under surveillance a few years previously. It still smelled of smoke but I was delighted with such a truly unique gift. Everyone was waiting for me to present my gift, but it wasn't forthcoming. There were a few grumblings around the room, before the music was cranked up again and the drinking resumed.

At midnight I had one last tradition to follow: climbing the 300-foot communications mast. The climb would be timed and that time recorded on a huge board in the Det bar. Matt Bleep currently held the record, set by him six months before. Typically with North Det, there was a twist: it had to be done naked. Everyone gathered outside the bar and I took my position at the base of the ladder. The air horn sounded and I began my climb. Flashbangs and smoke canisters were set off below for good measure as I made my way up the mast. I was by now a very experienced rigger but doing this naked was brutal and broke every health and safety rule in the book. Just as well I was too drunk to care.

I got to the top and the clock was stopped – I only just managed to scrape inside the top ten. Back in the bar, fully dressed this time, I had a few shots to warm myself up again. As it got later, more and more people came over to say good luck and good night before heading off. When I eventually got to bed myself, I set my alarm for only a few hours later. I had one last – top-secret – insertion job to do.

I woke later than planned at 0500 and headed straight for the tech bay. I put on my riggers harness and got what I needed from the boot of my car. I started my second climb of the day of the huge communications mast. My thighs were killing me and my head throbbed as I repeated the gruelling climb. I had to be quick again as it was getting light. I performed the insertion, taking in this view over the Foyle estuary one last time, and descended.

Once down, undetected, I jumped into my car and left North Det for good, planning to sleep off the effects of the night before parked somewhere on the road to Cork.

I was on the motorway just south of Dublin, when the phone rang. I hit the answer button on the hands-free and heard: 'You bastard! You bastard!' and a chorus of people laughing and shouting in the background. My leaving gift had found its mark. I knew the camp CO would be going off his nut and cursing the Det, but I didn't care. I had a good laugh picturing one of the lads scrambling up the mast to get it down.

For however brief a time, the Irish tricolour flew from the top of a 300-foot mast in one of most highly classified British army compounds in Northern Ireland. Written on it were the words, 'Ní bheidh ár leithéidí arís ann': The like of us will never be here again.

I hope it hangs now with the other North Det leaving gifts. I hope I will be remembered.

ACKNOWLEDGEMENTS

The journey to producing *Charlie One* didn't begin with the idea of producing a book at all but as a form of therapy. I had been diagnosed with PTSD a few years after leaving the British army. It was suggested by my therapist that writing down the thoughts that had plagued my life since leaving might exorcise some of those demons. For that, and so much more, I am indebted to Helen Callaghan. Before I knew it, some semblance of a book was forming. I say semblance, for that was all it was. It wasn't until I met my agent that the book started to take shape.

My sincere thanks to my publisher Conor Graham and his dynamic team at Merrion Press, namely Fiona Dunne, Katherine Kenny and Myles McCionnaith.

For my long-suffering family who have supported me without question through those darkest of days, I know there were often times when the burden seemed too great. I will never be able to express my gratitude to you for sticking by me. For my sister Sharon, my unofficial editor, who someday soon will publish her own work. For Kevin, Buddy and Ted, I always write better after the walk. For my own dog Missy, a constant companion and often source of motivation.

For the British army who undoubtedly gave me some of the best years of my life. I would wholeheartedly recommend it to anyone. The best of those days were at the Joint Communications Unit-Northern Ireland (JCU-NI). For my mates at North Det and Cameras Section, although it will never be officially acknowledged, you have helped to bring Northern Ireland to a better place. If there is anyone I have missed, and I'm sure there is, my thanks to you, too.

Finally, for my partner, Megan, who has put up with me throughout this journey. She is probably entitled to more of the proceeds from this book than I am, such has been her contribution. But let's not tell her that!